The Nature of Knowledge

The
Nature of
Knowledge

an introduction for librarians

by

D A KEMP

Senior Lecturer, Department of Librarianship
Newcastle-upon-Tyne Polytechnic

CLIVE BINGLEY
LONDON

LINNET BOOKS
HAMDEN · CONN

FIRST PUBLISHED 1976 BY CLIVE BINGLEY LTD
16 PEMBRIDGE ROAD LONDON W11 UK
SIMULTANEOUSLY PUBLISHED IN THE USA BY LINNET BOOKS
AN IMPRINT OF THE SHOE STRING PRESS INC
995 SHERMAN AVENUE HAMDEN CONNECTICUT 06514
SET IN 10 ON 12 POINT JOURNAL ROMAN
PRINTED IN GREAT BRITAIN BY OFFSET LITHOGRAPHY
BY BILLING & SONS LTD,
GUILDFORD, LONDON AND WORCESTER
COPYRIGHT © D A KEMP 1976
ALL RIGHTS RESERVED
BINGLEY ISBN: 0-85157-216-2
LINNET ISBN: 0-208-00000-0

Library of Congress Cataloging in Publication Data

Kemp, D   Alasdair
    The nature of knowledge.

    Bibliography: p.
    Includes index.
    1. Knowledge, Theory of. 2. Library science—Philosophy.
I. Title.
BD161.K45 1976   121   76-28343
ISBN 0-208-01528-0

CONTENTS

FOREWORD

by D J Foskett

I welcome this book, which makes an important contribution to progress in the intellectual analysis of the foundations of Library and Information Services. The growth of information service in libraries has led to a complete re-appraisal of the role of librarians in society, and their responsibilities in relation to all types of graphic records. We now recognise that we are past the days when our task was simply to buy and catalogue books, and produce them on request. The extension of these time-honoured crafts into the more positive activity of dissemination of knowledge and information leads us into the role of 'social memory', which in its turn requires a much more thorough acquaintance with the learning process in the individual, as well as the social processes of communication.

The work of contemporary philosophers, psychologists and sociologists therefore has direct relevance in the education and practice of librarians and information officers, and Mr Kemp has performed a thoroughly useful service in pointing up these inter-relations. By setting their contributions within the general framework of Systems Theory, he has produced a work which should guide the student, and the practising librarian, through a network of close and concentrated thinking, without difficulty. He has charted the field with clarity and precision, and his extensive bibliography provides a good starting point for those who will wish to carry on specialised studies in depth.

I hope, and expect that Mr Kemp's work will provide the necessary stimulus for others engaged in these professional activities, so that we may look forward to the establishment of a sound academic basis for the advancement of library and information science.

PREFACE

For some time now I have been teaching a course on knowledge and its communication in the Department of Librarianship at Newcastle-upon-Tyne Polytechnic, and this course appears in all the planned future syllabi of the department. Students have complained from the beginning that there is no textbook for the course, and the primary impetus for writing this text has been to fill that gap, although it covers only about half of this particular course.

The need arises because, although most of the ideas have appeared before, they are, inevitably, scattered throughout the literature of a wide variety of subjects, often in specialist publications which are not easy reading for the tyro. For this reason, too, many of the ideas have been recast and are illustrated by examples, rather than 'proved' by discussions of the data presented in the original publications. There are also some ideas in this text which have not been previously published—at least so far as I am aware; on one recent occasion, however, a student presented an essay citing a literature reference for what I had thought until then was my own original idea!

As well as providing a text for students, this book is an attempt to promote the concept that a full understanding of librarianship and information science involves an awareness of some, at least, of the other contributory branches of learning.

I have to thank my teaching colleagues for their encouragement and my wife and family for their forbearance. As one of their more demanding and exacting readers, it is pleasant to record the helpfulness of the staff and the excellence of the stocks of my polytechnic's library, without which this book could not have been written. I should also like to acknowledge the encouragement and criticism of my students: they have in various ways contributed a great deal to the content of this book. Notes provided by a former colleague, T D Wilson, gave me a headstart in developing my ideas. D J Foskett is due thanks for encouraging me to write this book, and Maurice Line encouraged me in the development of the course. Nevertheless, all the faults in the book are due entirely to me.

D A KEMP

Wylam, Northumberland
September 1975

Chapter 1

INTRODUCTION

This book is an attempt to discuss the nature and properties of knowledge. There are many other books on the subject, most of them longer
and more scholarly, and often written by men who have devoted a lifetime of study to the subject. There are only three excuses for adding
this book to their number. Firstly, it is sufficiently brief and unacademic
in its approach to be understandable, we hope, without a lifetime's study;
secondly it tries to encompass and bring together ideas from a number of
different fields of learning to make a text specifically for librarians; and
finally it discusses the problem in the context that knowledge exists not
only in the minds of people, but in books and other printed documents,
in films, maps, magnetic tapes and an ever-increasing host of forms which
may all be found on the shelves of libraries.

The importance of this record of knowledge cannot be over-estimated:
without it, the world as we know it would not and could not exist. It can
be claimed indeed that the collected knowledge on the shelves of the
world's libraries is both man's greatest achievement and his greatest possession (1).

If these arguments are accepted, then it becomes easy to press the case
for the inclusion of the study of the nature and properties of knowledge
in any course of education (2). A further educational advantage of such
study is that it requires some acquaintance at least with the methods,
aims and purposes of a number of different disciplines, and then attempts
to compare and combine their ideas.

The study of the nature and properties of the knowledge on his
shelves or in his computer is obviously particularly relevant to the student
of librarianship and information science, because it is, as it were, his
stock in trade. Without this study, the librarian or information scientist
is like a surgeon practised in operational techniques and equipment, who
knows nothing of the structure of the bodies on which he operates (3)
(4).

Libraries and information centres do not exist only as collectors of knowledge contained in documents; much more important, they strive to facilitate its communication. For this reason, the librarian or information scientist must know something of communication in general, of the creation and use of knowledge, and about the relationship of documented knowledge to other sorts. This book is not, however, concerned with the general aspects of communication, although where they impinge on the nature and properties of knowledge they cannot be overlooked (4).

The reader—who may think of libraries as 'sources of information'—might ask why this book is about 'knowledge' and not about 'information'. Inasmuch as the two terms are often used interchangeably, it is about information. On the other hand, the two terms are often contrasted, eg by Ziman, who refers to 'mere information' as opposed to knowledge. It is an important part of the argument of this text that if a distinction is made between knowledge and information, then the library is concerned with the former rather than the latter. In other words, libraries are 'sources of knowledge' rather than sources of information.

It is a concomitant of the exponential growth of knowledge, to which we refer in chapter 8, that the world is changing more rapidly than ever before (5). These changes affect the communication of knowledge, and therefore libraries, no less than any other area of human activity. At the present time two particular trends are affecting libraries. Firstly there is the rise of what (for lack of a better term) is referred to as the 'new media', and a corresponding decrease in the importance of the book as a source of information (6). The second is the increase in the power, availability and the comparative reduction in the cost of computer systems which can store and handle information, as well as a growing acceptance of them by the library profession (7).

This climate of change—and not just these two particular current examples—increases the need for an awareness of fundamentals and general principles, as contrasted with familiarity with details, for the latter are more subject to change than the former. For librarians as well as for information scientists, the study of knowledge and its communication can provide part of this essential awareness; it helps develop an understanding of *why* certain things are done, and it is only on the basis of such an understanding that it is possible to decide *how* to do them— how to meet needs and seize the new opportunities with which change will present the librarians and information scientists of the future (8).

So that the concepts can be referred to later in the text, a brief account of systems theory is given in chapter 2. Apart from their usefulness in this connection, these concepts are also part of the fundamental understanding just referred to. The examination of knowledge begins in chapter 3, in which the differences and relationships between the knowledge in the minds of individuals and the knowledge on the shelves of libraries is introduced. Chapter 3 concludes with an introduction to the content of the remainder of the text, to which the reader who wants such information is now referred.

It will be obvious from the foregoing that libraries cannot be regarded as stores of books, or even as collections of documents, however broadly the terms are defined, but instead as means for the communication of knowledge (9) (and entertainment, though these things are not necessarily separate). In this, and in the general tenor of this introduction, the knowledgeable reader will detect the influence of Jesse H Shera. The idea of distinguishing recorded knowledge was adopted from the ideas of Ziman, and has been developed further by ideas taken from the writings of Popper. A psychologist may also be able to detect the influence of Piaget (10). The ideas of numerous other authors also appear in this book, but the influence of those named has been crucial to the present author.

Many of the ideas included are theories which have been developed on the basis of experimental evidence, but in virtually every instance, rather than go into detail, and in order to make the ideas more easily understandable, imaginary or personal examples have been given.

The goals set out in the first paragraph of this introduction are very ambitious ones, and this book can only be regarded as a first step towards achieving them. I hope it is a step in the right direction, from which it will be possible to advance further.

NOTES AND REFERENCES
The full bibliographical citations are given in the bibliography at the end of the book (page 000).

1 Among others, Drucker (1969), Gray (1975), Innis (1964), ch 1 and 2, Magee (1973, p 61), Meredith (1956), Platt (1959), Sampson (1971, ch 5) and Shera (1972) discuss various aspects.

2 Gorn (1967).

3 The nature of information science or informatics is discussed by, among others, Brookes (1974), Caldwell (1970), Debons (1974), Foskett (1968) (1970), Gorn (1967), Kissel (1972), Line (1970), Mikhailov (1970), Otten (1970), Pohl (1965), Shera (1972), Stamper (1973, pt 1) (which is an account orientated away from libraries), Taylor (1973) and Wellisch (1972).

Papers concerned with the subject are collected in *Informatics* (1974), Mikhailov (1969) and Saracevic (1970).

4 Cherry (1966) is an excellent text dealing with very many aspects of communication—the innumerate reader should not be discouraged from examining the chapters which he can understand. An issue of *Scientific American* (Scientific American, 1972) deals with numerous aspects, is easier reading and more recent. Penland (1971) and McGarry (1975) are intended for librarians.

5 Toffler (1970) is a somewhat dramatic discussion of change. Handlin (1965) discusses the increasing pace of technological change and its effects. Eastlick (1971) is a collection of papers dealing with effects on libraries of social and technological change. Some of the references for chapter 8 are also relevant.

6 Innis (1964), Maddox (1972) and Taylor (1973). Wooster (1968) deals especially with scientific data, but his remarks apply to other fields which rely on data. An unpublished talk by B J Enright was a useful source of ideas.

7 These remarks are based on personal contacts, particularly on the changing attitudes and experiences of students.

8 Educational implications are discussed by Foskett (1973), Hayes (1969), Montgomery (1968), Shera (1972) and Taylor (1973).

9 The functions of libraries are discussed by Landheer (1957), Line (1970), Penland (1971), Saunders (1971) and Shera (1970) (1972).

10 Piaget (1972), Popper (1965) (1972), and Ziman (1968).

Chapter 2

THE PROPERTIES OF OPEN SYSTEMS

INTRODUCTION: A number of places in this book will refer to certain ideas as properties of systems (1). Knowledge itself, and 'society' which, as will be discussed in the next chapter and is a very important 'knower' in our context, may both be regarded as systems (2). For this reason it is necessary to devote a preliminary chapter to the general idea of systems and their properties.

The idea is also of increasing importance to those who are concerned with libraries and their management, so that the points in this chapter have wider implications that those connected with the later sections of the text. Much of the management theory which is being increasingly applied in libraries has its basis in the theory of systems, and the introduction of the use of computers to improve or reduce the cost of library services requires a detailed analysis of how the libraries actually operate; this analysis is also dependent on systems principles (3).

In an even wider context, the study of systems is an aid to the study of complex situations and organizations, in which it is not possible to make the problems easier by simply ignoring certain aspects, such as the fact that the situation being studied is continually changing, as for example in the case of growing plants. This fact may explain why the study of systems has its origins in biology, although it is now applied in many other areas such as sociology and technology (4). In turn, this wide range of applications is another reason for the importance of the systems concept. It provides a means whereby the problems in one area of study can be examined in the light of solutions found in another; it provides the framework of a common approach. For the reader of this text, this constitutes a third reason for the study of systems: the development of many of the ideas presented in it will require an increased understanding of a wide range of subjects.

The definition of 'systems'
Partly no doubt because of the numerous different applications of the systems idea, there are different definitions of systems, each of which

15

perhaps emphasizes certain aspects of importance to the particular context. The following is both sufficient for our purposes and provides a general consensus of (most of) the definitions:

a system is a whole or unity, comprised of interrelated and interdependent parts (or subsystems). The whole performs some 'function' to which each of the subsystems contributes by carrying out some 'operation', directly or indirectly related to the function of the whole.

Thus a polytechnic or university is a system, consisting of interrelated and interdependent departments. Its function is the propagation (in several senses) of knowledge; the departments carry out operations such as research, teaching and examining (directly related to the function), and administration (indirectly related to the function, but essential for the survival of the polytechnic or university).

All of the systems with which we are concerned (arguably, indeed, all systems) are 'open' systems. This means that they absorb 'input', in the form of energy or materials from the outside (the 'environment' or 'supersystem') and return 'output', which almost always takes a different form from the input. Indeed, the function of open systems may be described generally as the transformation of input from the environment and its subsequent transferral back into the environment. Usually, too, the output takes the form of the intended 'product' (which may be intangible, in the case of systems which perform a service), and also of 'waste', the unwanted but unavoidable results of the process of transformation.

These ideas can be represented diagrammatically. In Figures 1 and 2 respectively, we show a general diagram, and a diagram of the ideas applied to a polytechnic as a teaching system. We make here the general point that the use of diagrams, of several different kinds, is a feature of the discussion and application of systems ideas.

Systems, supersystems and subsystems

In the foregoing we have used the terms 'subsystem', 'system' and 'supersystem' or 'environment'. It is necessary however to realize that these terms are relative; we may, for example, be interested in polytechnics and decide to regard a polytechnic as a system, in which case the 'community served' may, as in figure 2, be assumed as the supersystem, and the polytechnic library is an example of a subsystem. On the other hand, it is possible to regard either the community served by the polytechnic, or the polytechnic library, as systems. In these cases, the polytechnic is respectively a subsystem of the community; or the supersystem or environment in which the polytechnic library functions.

16

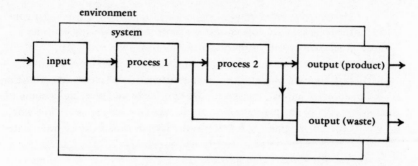

Figure 1: General system

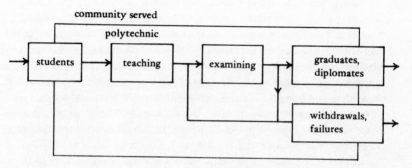

Figure 2: A polytechnic as a teaching system

In connection with supersystems, it can be noted that a system may be thought of as belonging to more than one supersystem or environment; this is the idea of 'partial inclusion'. Therefore in the case of polytechnics, the supersystem is the community served: however there is another super-system, namely the general educational system of the country. The fact of their inclusion in both these supersystems is important for and to poly-technics (and the situation may of course be rather more complex, because several supersystems may be involved).

The interest in the environment in which the system under discussion exists and functions is one of the features (and advantages) of the systems approach. The realization that systems are dependent on the environment and are affected by their interaction with it is frequently a considerable improvement on a simple 'common-sense' approach.

Several different kinds of subsystems can be distinguished according to the kind of operation they carry out; these, however, need not concern us here.

17

Properties of open systems

In the following we concentrate on those properties of systems in general relevant to our further discussions. There are some properties which are quite general, and others which are possessed by systems of particular kinds. In biology, for example, where the system discussed is a plant or an animal, the system has definite boundaries, and something is either part of the plant, or not. In the case of social systems, however, one of their distinguishing features is the lack of such boundaries.

Organisation and its implications

As the very name implies, systems are organised. They do not consist of unorganised collections of identical objects, but of organisations of subsystems which can be distinguished from each other, and which are, as the definition states, inter-related and interdependent. Only a marginal difference is made to a bag of marbles if they all change places in the bag, or if one of their number is lost. If, however, the administrative unit or the library of a polytechnic were to change position or disappear, such changes would have major repercussions on the polytechnic as a whole, and on all the subsystems within it. In technical terms, systems have 'negative entropy'—they are organised *This is true of open systems; closed systems possess 'entropy' or the tendency for their parts to become disorganised and indistinguishable from each other (5).

In a sense, however, organisation is not a 'natural' state. Left to themselves, things naturally cease to be organised and become more and more disorganised. (Without going into any technical detail we can point out that this is a fundamental principle in nature: the second law of thermodynamics.) In order to maintain the distinctiveness of subsystems and the relationships between them, that is to maintain its organised quality, the system must use 'energy'. ('Energy' in the present context can mean energy in the narrow sense, such as electrical power, or 'manpower'. It may also mean materials such as the paper which is necessary for the organisation of any large social system such as a polytechnic.) This energy must be acquired from outside the system; the system is therefore dependent for its continued organisation and thus its continued existence, on input from the environment. This is the fundamental reason for the dependence of systems on their environments, mentioned earlier, and which is a very important property of systems.

Another property of systems follows on from their property of dependence on their environments: this is that systems are dependent on information about their environments, particularly but not only in the case of

18

social systems. They are in technical terms dependent on 'information input'. This is distinct from other kinds of input, in exactly the sense that finding out where one's next meal is coming from is different from actually eating. A polytechnic must, for example, have information about changes in the community which it serves, so that it can adjust to them. As an example, if the community is to expand its social services, the polytechnic must have information about this, so that it can prepare itself to undertake the education of the increased numbers of social workers which will be required by the community. Much of the information input to systems is 'feedback'—information about the reaction of the environment to the system and its products or output. An example of negative feedback in the case of a polytechnic would be information about the inability of certain of its graduates to perform the tasks for which they were supposed to have been educated and trained. In such a case the information would be necessary in order that the education and training could be changed. (One hastens to add that this is a hypothetical example.) (6).

Growth and its consequences

Systems have the property of tending to increase in size—to grow. All systems, with the possible exception of technological systems (which 'grow' in another rather different sense), pass through a stage of growth (7). When they reach their optimal 'best possible' size, many systems then acquire the ability of maintaining their equilibrium. It is this property of growth, and the properties which systems possess in their growing stage which are of greatest interest to us.

The first of these properties is that of increasing differentiation: as a system increases in size, its subsystems become increasingly unlike each other in form and in the operations which they perform. A small college will have a small administration and most of the staff in the administrative department will be able to perform a number of different tasks—enrol students, keep their records, obtain supplies, obtain and make payments, etc. When the college becomes larger, the administration will also become larger, simply because there will be more administrative work to do. It will also—and this is the important point—become more differentiated within itself. There might, for example, be a section concerned with the enrolment of students and the maintenance of their records; one whose function it is to obtain supplies; another which deals with finance (when

19

the system gets even bigger this will develop separate and different sub-sections concerned with payments and receipts); and so on. Another way of expressing the same idea, particularly in the context of social systems, is that there is increasing specialisation—instead of a few people 'specialising' in administration, there will be a larger number of people each with a much more restricted range of responsibilities and duties. Consequently, it will become increasingly difficult for the individual to perform the duties (operations) of another member of the organisation. When, for example, there is both a purchasing section and a finance section within an administrative unit, it becomes impossible for a person to transfer from one to the other without a degree of retraining; whereas, in a smaller and less differentiated unit, duties and responsibilities are more easily transferred because they have already been shared.

This leads onto another consequence of the growth of systems. As it increases in size, the system tends to become more complex: not only are the subsystems themselves more distinct and differentiated, but also the relationships between them necessarily become more complicated. The pattern that this evolving complexity takes in growing social systems is a fascinating study in its own right. As a very simple example, in the enlarging administration previously referred to, the original administration would have a structure consisting, perhaps, of one person in charge, and the rest sharing the work as and when it arose. As the system and administration grew, this method would have been replaced by the specialist sections and subsections referred to earlier, and also by a series of levels—a hierarchy—in which individuals were responsible to and for other individuals and groups of individuals. Certain members therefore are likely to find that, by the very nature of their operations, they are responsible to more than one person. If that seems complex, the intention will be served; large systems are complex (and systems theory is a method for sorting out their complexities).

As a corollary of the previous point it may be noted that the relationships between subsystems of a social system tend to become more formal as the system grows larger. In a small organisation it may be possible to pass on information simply by word of mouth; when the organisation becomes larger, memoranda may be needed; while the largest organisations find it necessary to publish some kind of newsletter in order to ensure that communication is successfully and effectively achieved.

The final property of systems which we should consider is the cyclical nature of the events which take place; indeed, systems may be regarded as cycles of events. This means that a system takes in input, processes or

20

transforms it and passes it out to the environment—as has been described. The output, however, is used and re-modified in some way by the environment (or by some system within it) and directly or indirectly it is then possible for the environment to make available further input to the first system. Perhaps the most famous of these cycles is the biological nitrogen one, in which nitrogen is passed from plants to animals to the soil and thence back to plants; being at each stage transformed into different compounds, which are the form in which the next stage can use the nitrogen as input. The same cyclical property can be seen in lending libraries, where books lent are output and books returned are input. At a more complicated level, the books and the knowledge in them are output: the knowledge is used and transformed by authors into further books which then form the input to the library, which are then used by other authors . . . (figure 3).

Summary and conclusions

In this chapter, we have tried to show the relevance of the concept of systems, and to discuss those properties of systems to which we shall refer later. Only a very few examples have been given and those have mostly been of social systems.

It is, however, important to realise that in every case other examples of the property could have been given from systems of other kinds: from physical systems such as the Solar System, from biological systems such as plants and animals, and from non-human social systems, such as swarms of bees. Examples could also have been related very easily to a wide range of social systems, all different in size, content and structure. Extending the range of examples in this way would perhaps convince the reader of the general applicability of the systems idea, and it is suggested that he may care to try to find examples for himself.

It must also be admitted that in this brief account we cannot claim to have summarised all that has been written about systems; only some of the properties of systems have been discussed, some have been merely mentioned and a few have been ignored altogether. We have tried to make it clear that among the properties of any entity said to be a system, the following appear:

organisation: unless the components are organised (and interrelated and interdependent) there is no system;

input: in order to maintain its organised state (and in order to produce its 'product') the system requires the input of 'energy';

dependence on the environment is implied by the need for input; no (open) system can exist in isolation from its surroundings;

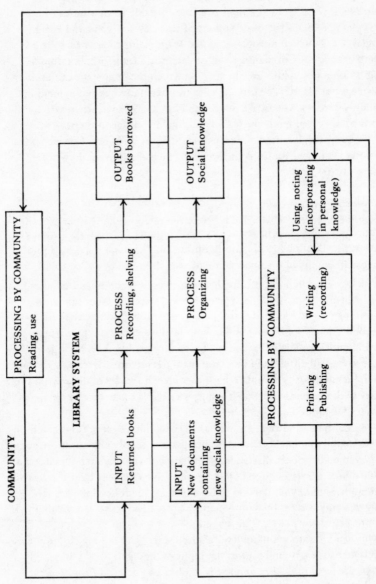

Figure 3: The top cycle is the lending library cycle. The bottom cycle shows how knowledge is processed and re-processed (the terms personal knowledge, social knowledge and recording are discussed in chapter 3).

information input: dependence on the environment implies the need for information about it; such information must be input to the system;

growth: in one sense or another, all systems undergo growth stages, during which there also occur

increasing differentiation: the subsystems become increasingly unlike each other; they become increasingly specialized;

increasing complexity: relationships between subsystems become more and more involved;

cycles of events: systems are dependent on the environment for their input and to which they return their output; the environment uses the output, and this leads (sometimes through a complicated chain of events) to the availability of further input for the system. The process (or processes) are continuously repeated in a circulatory or cyclical manner.

NOTES AND REFERENCES

1   This account is based mainly on Katz (1966), especially chapters 2 and 6, some of which have been reprinted in Emery (1969) and Grusky (1970).

Churchman (1968) is introductory and contains a section on libraries (p 104-125). Beishon (1971) and Beishon (1972), which is a selection of readings, are intended for undergraduate use. Bertalanffy (1962) and Boulding (1956) are standard references, much reprinted, eg in Beishon (1972) and Buckley (1968). Laszlo (1972) has been recommended by Foskett (1974). Klir (1972) is not recommended for student use, although it is interesting. Bertalanffy (1968) is the comprehensive account by the doyen of systems theory.

2   Knowledge as a system is discussed by Blachowicz (1971), Buckley (1972), Cigànik (1969) and Weiss (1960), the last probably being the best introduction. See also note 5.

3   Systems ideas in relation to libraries and information systems are discussed by Bergen (1966), Foskett (1972) (1974), Reyward (1969), Swanson (1970) and Vickery (1973), the last being a textbook. Liston (1971) discusses the use of system ideas in the design of information systems, while practical accounts of their use in relation to libraries appear in Robinson (1969) and Thomas (1971), as well as in any decent textbook on library mechanization, eg Kimber (1974).

Katz (1966) is a standard reference for systems in management courses. Systems ideas in relation to management theory are criticised by Silverman (1974) whose comments do not, however, affect the content of this chapter.

4   Lotka (1925) was one of the original creators.

5 Entropy is discussed by Angrist (1973) and in Cherry (1966, p 51ff and p 306) and in a wide variety of other references. For entropy and 'knowledge systems' see Fugmann (1972), Hall (1959), and especially Kelley (1969), although none of these is easy reading.

6 The idea of feedback, and particularly of negative feedback, is discussed in most of the texts referred to. Milsum (1968) discusses also positive feedback, a concept whose importance to social systems (and therefore libraries) may have been underemphasised in the past.

7 See especially Weiss (1960).

Chapter 3

THE NATURE OF KNOWLEDGE

INTRODUCTION: The first purpose of this chapter is to make a basic distinction between two different kinds of knowledge. This distinction is fundamental to the approach taken in subsequent chapters to the study of the nature of knowledge, and the second purpose of the chapter is to outline this approach and the reasons for it.

Social and personal knowledge

It is possible to put forward the idea that there is quite a large number of different kinds of knowledge. This approach to examining the nature of knowledge is discussed in chapter 10, *The universe of knowledge.* We may, however, consider knowledge as being only of two basic types: 'social knowledge' and 'personal knowledge' (1).

Personal knowledge, which might also be called private knowledge, is the knowledge held in the mind of an individual, and as such is available only to him, or through him, *ie* by asking him questions. Until comparatively recently, the study of the nature of knowledge was almost entirely concerned with knowledge of this kind.

Social knowledge (or 'public knowledge') is the knowledge possessed collectively by a society or social system; it is available freely and equally to all members of that society through its records. The important distinction between these two different kinds of knowledge lies, therefore, in the question of availability. Because social knowledge is, in principle, available through consultation of the records to all members of the society, it is that kind of knowledge which is to be found in libraries, and its nature is of considerable importance to librarians. Nevertheless, this does not preclude an interest in personal knowledge, for reasons to be explained.

At this point we must note that the alternative terms 'private knowledge' and 'public knowledge' are also used by philosophers to express a difference between kinds of knowledge, and are used by them with rather different meanings from those used in the present text. The question is discussed later (p 37ff).

Two brief comments on the notions of records and public availability may usefully be interjected here. Firstly they imply documents and writing of some sort, and therefore a literate society. Social anthropologists might well feel that the definition of social knowledge which we have given is not valid for all societies; however it can be justified for all societies which have need of libraries (see also p 91). It should also be noted that the society is not necessarily a political unit: eg in the case of records of mathematical knowledge, the society could be considered to be the world's mathematicians. Secondly, in modern society, 'recording' does not merely mean writing something down. It implies also having it published in some form such as books, which are to be found in libraries; so that it will be available, not only to the person who writes it down, but to all members of the society (compare the bottom cycle on figure 3 in chapter 2).

Although we have made a very clearcut division between personal and social knowledge, it is necessary to clarify that the distinction is one of degree rather than absolute dichotomy. Thus, there exists in most societies, a large amount of what may conveniently be called 'semi-social knowledge'. We have stated that social knowledge exists in records equally and freely available to all members of the society which possesses the knowledge. There will, however, exist in the society, records which are not always available—and which are not intended to be available—to all members of the society. One relevant example is what are often referred to as 'semi-published' documents; these are principally reports prepared by or for government bodies. They may be quite widely available, in some cases being distinguished in practice only by the fact that they have to be obtained from different sources from those of ordinary published documents. At the other extreme, they may be available only to a very limited few. Another example is the records which are properly the concern of only a particular subsystem of society: personnel records, bank accounts, income tax returns and the like, may all be regarded as semi-social knowledge. The extent to which knowledge is to be regarded as social or semi-social depends on the extent to which the records containing it are available to all.

The suggestion that an individual's personal knowledge must all be in his head may be an over-simplification: his private correspondence and the notes which he may make are also part of his personal knowledge. Thus, the notes on which this chapter is based may be seen as part of the author's personal knowledge: they are not available to others, in that other people could not easily find them;

and if they were found it could not be guaranteed that they would be understood. The same remark may apply to notes being made by the reader.

In defining social knowledge, we stated that it must be available by consulting records: this does not mean, however, that the records must always be consulted before such knowledge is available and used: if anything the reverse is true. The geography of our home towns is social knowledge because it is available in the street plans and maps which can be consulted in libraries and purchased from bookshops. However, we did not learn it that way, but from what we were told and shown, and from our own experience. Indeed, much of what constitutes social knowledge is learned before the members of the society to whom it is available are able to consult the records in which it is embodied: it is learnt 'at mother's knee'. The ability to use the language of the society is perhaps the primary example.

The relationship between social and personal knowledge

It is obvious that the definitions given of social and personal knowledge are not intended to imply that they are mutually exclusive. Much knowledge is of course both 'social' and 'personal', as is the geography of our home towns, to which we have just referred.

Indeed, it is true to say that all social knowledge has at some time been the personal knowledge of an individual: new ideas and new facts, ie new knowledge, can only originate in the minds of people (see also p 76). As an example we may take the case of Newton's work on the laws of gravity. All the ideas which contributed to his development of the laws (excluding perhaps the apocryphal apple) were available in publications. It was only in someone's mind, however, that the laws could be created; in this case it was in the mind of Newton (2). But we must note that to have an idea only contributes to the *personal* knowledge of the individual who has it. For it to become social knowledge it must, by definition, be recorded and be made publicly available.

It is also possible to state that social knowledge is an essential source of personal knowledge. The individual cannot know of all social knowledge: there is now simply too much to know, to learn and to remember. Nor can the individual hope to be able to find out from other people, because it would take him too long to find the people who know. In modern society, access to records, to social knowledge, is essential. This, it should be emphasised, is true not only of academic or 'book' learning, but also of everyday life. Thus the records most often used are things

like timetables. These relationships between personal and social knowledge are illustrated in figure 1, which may be compared with the bottom
cycle of figure 3 in chapter 2. The size of the circles in the diagram is
not representative, nor is the area of overlap.

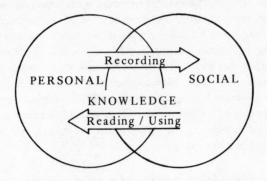

Figure 1: The relationship between personal and social knowledge

The approach to the study of knowledge
In the examination of the nature of knowledge in the following chapters, two different kinds of knowledge will be considered separately, first
personal knowledge, and then social knowledge.

Social knowledge is the librarian's stock in trade: it is, by and large,
what libraries contain (although a number of libraries actively deal also
with semi-social knowledge, in the form of reports, etc). As has been
described, however, social knowledge originates as personal knowledge:
the latter is the source of the former. Again, social knowledge is a source
of personal knowledge, being either learned directly in order to expand
the individual's personal knowledge as in the case of those endeavouring
to learn from textbooks, or else being used as a source of existing ideas
which the individual uses to create and formulate new ideas of his own—
that is, to create new knowledge.

Thus, although librarians are concerned with social knowledge, they
must also be concerned with personal knowledge; they ought to know
how social knowledge comes into existence and how it is used. This is
one reason for the study of personal knowledge. Another reason is that
personal knowledge serves as a paradigm or model for social knowledge:
properties possessed by personal knowledge may well be expected to
reveal themselves also in social knowledge (3).

28

In our study of personal knowledge, we examine ideas from two branches of learning: philosophy and psychology. Philosophy is the oldest branch of learning to concern itself with the nature of knowledge. The science of psychology derived from philosophy, but uses a rather different approach in its consideration of the nature of knowledge. We also consider briefly some physiological theories about how the brain may work, and compare them with a potential development in methods of recording social knowledge and making it available. This approach will be used again later.

The examination of social knowledge begins by considering scientific knowledge, which may be regarded as the model of social knowledge. We therefore discuss the method whereby scientific knowledge is created, the philosophy which underlies the method, and the properties of the knowledge produced. Then attention can be turned to the relation of our ideas of social knowledge to similar, though not identical, ideas which have been put forward by other writers.

We next consider the evidence from social psychology about factors in a society which may affect the social knowledge in its possession. Then we consider the growth of knowledge, considering reasons, measurements and implications of its growth. Finally we consider the possibility of the existence of different kinds of knowledge (apart from the social and personal kinds just discussed) and whether and how the existence of different kinds of knowledge might affect its organisation and use.

What has been learnt from our examination of these various different approaches to the study of knowledge will then be reviewed with an attempt to draw some conclusions.

NOTES AND REFERENCES

1 The basis of this approach is formed by the ideas of Popper and Ziman, which are discussed in chapter 6. For another discussion see Kemp (1974).

2 Mason (1956) p 157-163. This example is particularly apt.

3 A further aspect is user psychology: see Foskett (1970) (1972), Garvey (1974), Kemp (1974) and Line (1970). More generally, see Penland (1971).

Chapter 4

PHILOSOPHY AND KNOWLEDGE

INTRODUCTION: Philosophy is a form of study which is difficult to define. It means, or has meant, different things to different people at different times. For example, Chinese philosophy is different from Indian philosophy; Anglo-American philosophy is different from continental European philosophy. Two thing are, perhaps, characteristic of the kind of philosophy with which we are concerned: its purpose, which may be called a search for ultimate truths, and its methods, which consist of thought and discussion.

The kind of ultimate truths with which philosophy is concerned include the meanings and definitions of such sentences as 'I may', and, of particular interest to us, 'I know'. (Obviously, these expressions have commonsense meanings, or it would be impossible to use them in everyday life. The philosopher, however, is not concerned with everyday usage, but with an analysis to provide an indisputable meaning.) The methods may be briefly demonstrated by considering the response of a typical scientist, detective, historian, and philosopher to the challenge 'prove it'. The scientist, the detective and the historian would each in his different way try to find evidence: the scientist by devising some experiment, the detective perhaps by visiting the scene of the crime, and the historian by examining documents in some archive or library. This search for evidence is just what the philosopher typically would *not* do. His response would be to think out additional arguments about why it was correct, and to find counter-arguments to refute the propositions of those who argued differently from him. If he wanted evidence to illustrate his points, he would merely refer to whatever was happening outside his window, or recount some experience from his everyday life. (This evidence would, however, be used only as illustration, and not as proof).

The branch of philosophy which is concerned with the nature of knowledge is called 'epistemology' derived from the Greek word *episteme*, which can be approximately translated as 'knowledge'. In our examination of the philosophical approach to the nature of knowledge, the ideas of Ayer, Austin and Popper will be considered. (In the case of Popper we return to his ideas in the context of the philosophy of science, in chapter 6 (1).) We shall also consider ideas about sources of, and different kinds of, knowledge; ideas to which we return when dealing with the universe of knowledge, in chapter 10.

Knowledge versus true opinion

One way of examining the nature of knowledge is to consider what a person means when he says 'I know'. What are the implications of this statement? Can its meaning be analysed in such a way as to provide us with a definition of knowledge? Consider the following example. The writer might say, 'It is my opinion that most of my students will pass the examinations.' To this may be added the fact that this opinion is almost certainly correct. In other words:

a) I have an opinion, *and*

b) my opinion is correct (true).

Now it can be argued that both of these statements are also implied when I say 'I know'. Here are two more examples:

1 I may say,

a) 'It is my opinion that Sunderland Football Club is in the Football League'

and (let us suppose) this opinion is correct, that in reality

b) it is true that Sunderland FC is in the Football League.

2 I may say,

'I know that Sunderland FC is in the Football League',

thereby implying

a) it is my opinion that Sunderland FC is in the Football League, *and*

b) it is true that Sunderland FC is in the Football League.

Philosophers, or at least some of them, have tried to discuss the nature of knowledge by comparing an opinion or belief which is (or which happens to be) true, as in example 1, with knowledge (or with a claim to have knowledge), as in example 2. The approach is, therefore, known as the question of knowledge versus true opinion. What they have done is to attempt to find a third statement which could be made in the case of example 2, where 'I know' was used, but which would not apply in the case of example 1, where 'It is my opinion' was used. We shall refer to this third statement as c, as it follows from a and b. Various candidates for the third statement have been proposed and these can now be considered.

Adequate evidence

One idea for the third statement would be to say that:

c) 'I have adequate evidence for the fact that Sunderland FC is in the Football League.'

In commonsense—and perhaps in law—this may perhaps be acceptable. To a philosopher, however, it is not sufficient; because, on examination, the statement 'I have adequate evidence that' always ultimately implies my saying, 'I know'. Thus the evidence which I put forward in this case could be the tables of League clubs in my newspapers last Sunday. But this would imply that 'I know' about the accuracy of my Sunday news-papers—which would entail finding adequate evidence for my knowing about their accuracy—and so on.

Observation

In this case, the third statement is of the nature of:

c) such and such has been observed; *for example*

c) Sunderland FC has been observed to be in the Football League.

This approach is often adopted by philosophers of science, and, again, it seems to be satisfactory in a commonsense sort of way, especially if one considers it to be a kind of transformation of the old adage 'seeing is believing' ('observing is knowing'). Yet again, however, it is not satis-factory to a philosopher.

Among their reasons for not accepting it are the following. Firstly, some knowledge does not depend on observation at all, but on reasoning. Logical propositions (such as 'If A equals B, and if B equals C, then A equals C'), and mathematics generally, do not rely on observation but on the use of reason. Secondly, it can be argued that observation itself always depends on knowledge. For example, I cannot observe cows in terms of their being (say) largish animals with four legs, a tail and udders, unless 'I know' what animals, legs, tails and udders are; and so on. To most people, a radar screen simply shows dots and smudges, but to a trained observer—whose training has given him the appropriate knowledge—these dots and smudges represent aircraft, clouds, flocks of birds, etc, moving in certain directions at certain speeds. Unless we know what we are observing, we cannot observe it. This point is also re-examined in the context of psychology (p 47), and there are also further philosophical aspects which we need not go into here.

Probability

Another possibility for the third statement is that:

c) it is probable that such and such is the case; *for example*

c) it is probable that Sunderland FC is in the Football League.
The first thing to do is to consider what probable (or probability) means
here. Firstly, there is probability in the statistical sense. We examine
this concept later (p 70) but ignore it now, on the grounds that statistical probability includes the notion that there is no such thing as
dead certainty; and, therefore, it seems that if this does not exist, then
we cannot even make statement b, because we cannot be certain about
it. The second use of 'probability' is related to the idea of evidence, and
the use of reasoning from evidence. Thus:

c) this is probable, *because* Sunderland FC regularly plays other teams
   in the Football League.

This idea, however, raises the objection about adequate evidence. In
order to be able to give reasons, we must *know* the evidence for those
reasons. In this example, at the time of writing, the 'other teams'
would include Hull City FC, so that the evidence implies the statement:

'I know that Hull City FC is in the Football League.'
This changes the Football Club concerned, but does not get us any nearer
to discovering what 'I know' means.

Another sense of probability which may be distinguished is called 'absolute probability'—the equivalent of what we mean when we use the phrase
'in all probability'. For example:

c) in all probability, Sunderland FC is in the Football League.
What we are doing in making this kind of statement is saying that something is more probably true than not, in relation to certain statements
which we claim to know. (It may be that we ourselves do not claim to
know them, but that we are willing to accept the evidence of others,
whom, perhaps, we consider to be experts, *eg* the football correspondents
in our Sunday newspapers.) It seems to me that we may substitute for
'in all probability' in our latest candidate for statement c, the expression
'it (or things) make(s) sense if . . .' or 'it is reasonable to believe that . . .'.
For example:

c) things make sense if Sunderland FC is in the Football League; *or*
c) it is reasonable to believe that Sunderland FC is in the Football
   League.

This brings us back to the problem of evidence—because the things referred to must be evidence, or ideas which we can give as grounds for
reasoning. They also raise the question of how we can reason—how we
can draw justifiable conclusions from particular starting points or premises.
These problems are discussed by philosophers, but because it is claimed
for scientific knowledge that it is based on evidence and reasoning, they

are particularly important in regard to that kind of knowledge, and we shall therefore discuss them in that context (p 71 ff). We must, however, point out that the notion of probability (or the similar notion of 'reasonableness') can both be regarded as philosophically unsatisfactory because they involve the idea of evidence, which itself may be shown to be unsatisfactory.

The arguments that the statement 'I know' (and therefore the nature of knowledge) can be distinguished or defined in terms of the foregoing notions of adequate evidence, observation or probability, may all be regarded as inadequate, because on examination they all rely, ultimately, on the ability to say 'I know'.

Knowledge as 'the right to know'

Another rather different proposition is that the third statement has the form that the knower 'has the right to know' that such and such is the case, for example:

c) I [being an ardent follower of Sunderland FC] have the right to know that Sunderland FC is in the Football League; or

c) I [being the manager of Sunderland FC] have the right to know that Sunderland FC is in the Football League.

Note that the word 'right' has the word 'duty' as a concomitant:

c) I [being the manager of Sunderland FC] have the duty to know that Sunderland FC is in the Football League.

This seems a commonsense argument: if the manager of Sunderland FC does not know whether the club is in the Football League, who else can be expected to know? Ayer puts this idea forward as the philosophically most satisfactory of the third statements; but, nevertheless, counterarguments can be brought forward, by asking what is meant by 'right' and 'duty'. This takes us into the discussion of the philosophy of ethics: suffice it to say that it is as difficult to define 'right' and 'duty' as it is to define 'knowledge'.

Other approaches to the nature of knowledge

Not all philosophers agree that the attempt to discover a third statement which represents the difference between knowledge and true opinion is the best, or even a useful, approach to the problem of attempting to define knowledge or to discover its properties. They argue that the difference between knowledge and true opinion either is not essential or does not exist. Two modern examples of this view in Britain are the approaches of J L Austin and Sir Karl Popper.

Performative utterances

We might say that when a person uses the expression 'I know' he is intending to inform his audience about two things:

1   about his state of mind in relation to some idea, *and*
2   about the relation of that state of mid to the reality of the situation.

For example, if I were to say,

'I know that Sunderland FC is in the Football League', I would be trying to tell you two things:

1   my impression or understanding of the situation is that Sunderland FC is in the Football League; *and*
2   that my understanding of the situation is correct—Sunderland FC *is* in the Football League.

Austin suggests that this interpretation of the use of the expression 'I know' amounts to saying that when a person uses it he is *giving a report:* firstly, about the state of his mind, or understanding; and secondly, about the relationship of that state, or understanding, to the reality. Austin himself, however, argues that when a person says 'I know' his intention is *not* to do this, *ie* it is *not* the intention to give a report. Rather, it is the intention of the person concerned to give his guarantee, to give his 'word', that such and such is the case. For example, were I to say,

'I know that Sunderland FC is in the Football League',

I would not be concerned (according to Austin) to report to you on my understanding of the situation, or on its relation to reality: rather I am saying, or implying, that:

'I give you my guarantee that Sunderland FC is in the Football League.' In support of this idea he compares the expression 'I know', with the expression 'I promise'. When a person says 'I promise' he is not making a statement, he is carrying out an action: the action of giving his promise to an audience. If, for example, the manager of Sunderland FC (at the time of writing in the Second Division of the Football League) says to a supporter,

'I promise that Sunderland FC will be in the First Division next season',

he is not, and cannot be, making a report about a fact, because the fact lies in the future and cannot be reported; what he is doing is giving his promise. A similar comparison can be made with other verbs, notably 'I command'. The argument put forward is that when a person says,

'I promise', *or*

'I command',

he is not stating something; rather, he is doing something. Austin claims that these expressions may, therefore, be regarded as what he calls 'performative utterances'; expressions whose purpose is not to convey information but to do something. His argument is that 'I know' belongs to this class of performative utterances: when we use that expression, we are performing the act of giving our guarantee. His idea is not accepted by all philosophers, some of whom take the contrary view that when a person says 'I know', he is in fact simply reporting on the state of his mind.

The importance of truth

We shall be examining the ideas of Sir Karl Popper in some detail later, but for the moment we may note that he does not believe that there is any point in searching for a third statement in the way we have been discussing. He suggests that the nub of the matter lies in the second statement, 'It is true that . . .' Popper says that the important point about knowledge is whether it is true or not. The real test of any knowledge about Sunderland FC and the Football League is whether Sunderland FC is in the Football League—or not. If it is, I know it: if it is not in, I do not (and cannot) know it. His arguments may be related to the idea of reasonableness discussed earlier.

Sources of knowledge

A completely different approach to the problem of defining knowledge is to ask two questions:

1 What do we know?

That is, what is the extent of our knowledge? How much can we know?

2 How can we decide that we know anything?

That is, what criteria can be used in deciding that something is knowledge? The discussion of these points is too involved to be dealt with briefly, but one aspect is particularly relevant. This is the question of 'sources of knowledge'—where does the knowledge that we have come from? More precisely:

1 Are there any sources from which knowledge can be drawn?

2 Is it possible to regard these as valid?

There is not complete agreement on this, but there are four principal candidate sources: external perception, apperception, memory and reason.

External perception is put forward as the source of our knowledge of the 'external world', *ie* of knowledge which we gain through our senses of seeing, hearing, feeling, *etc.* The study of the process of perception has been taken up by philosophers of science and by psychologists and it will be examined again in that context, in the next chapter.

Apperception is the source of our knowledge about ourselves, about our 'inner being'—our emotions. It is sometimes referred to as inner consciousness or self-awareness. Memory is the source of our knowledge of the past: like perception, this is a question which has been taken up by psychologists, and which we examine in that context. Reason is the source of rational truths or logic (such as the A equals B, B equals C, etc, example given earlier). We shall also examine an aspect of this (the 'problem of induction') later, in relation to the philosophy of science (p 71ff).

As well as these four sources, some philosophers propose others. Of these, it is especially relevant to a later discussion to mention faith, which may be the source from which religious or spiritual knowledge is drawn. (If we were to ask a priest to 'prove it', as in the example at the beginning of this chapter, his reply would be to the effect that neither he nor anyone else *can* prove it: the enquirer must just have faith. He might then tell him how to go about acquiring that faith. We return to this notion of the sources of knowledge in dealing with the idea of *The universe of knowledge* in chapter 10.

Public and private knowledge

In the introduction to our study of the nature of knowledge in the previous chapter, a distinction was made between 'social knowledge' and 'personal knowledge', and we noted that 'public knowledge' and 'private knowledge' respectively could be used as alternative terms. The terms 'public knowledge' and 'private knowledge' are also used by philosophers in connection with two of the sources of knowledge. There is a clear difference however between the way in which in this book the terms social knowledge and personal knowledge are used, and the use of the terms 'public knowledge' and 'private knowledge' by philosophers (2). There is also a subtle relationship between the two pairs of ideas, which is due to their evolution. To examine the point here is, however, confusing, complicated, and unnecessary.

We mentioned that in philosophical terms, perception is the source of knowledge of the external world, that is the world which we perceive through our senses. Knowledge of that sort has the property that it can be communicated absolutely. A modern philosopher of science would certainly dispute this statement, but at least for the moment we shall pass over the comments he would be likely to make (see also p 74). For example, a tree is part of my external world: I can say 'tree' and you will know exactly what I mean. Apperception is the source of knowledge about ourselves, of our inner beings—of our emotional feelings. Knowledge of this sort is unlike knowledge of the external world, because it cannot be communicated fully: there is, for example, no means by which I can describe just exactly how I feel when I am angry. I can say that I am angry, and you can think of how you feel when you are angry and assume that my present state is similar to that one; but you can never *know exactly* my feelings when I am angry. The cause of this difference is that I can point out a tree (this is the process of denotation referred to on p 54), but I cannot point out to you my inner feelings of anger, because they are inside me. Because it *can* be pointed out in this way, our knowledge of the external world is 'objective' or 'public'—public because it can be communicated. Conversely, our knowledge of ourselves is 'subjective', or 'private'—private because it *cannot* be communicated fully.

It is important to realise that this represents the philosopher's use and understanding of these terms. Later, when we examine how psychologists view knowledge, it will be seen that a person's knowledge tends to be an amalgam of public, objective knowledge (denotations is the term used in that context), and of private, subjective knowledge (connotations). It is also worth noting that writers on philosophy and psychology sometimes use these terms to express ideas which are different, although related, and also that terms such as 'extensional' and 'intensional', and 'informative' and 'affective' are used in the same or slightly different interpretations (see also p 55-6). Whenever the reader comes across them, he is advised to check on the exact sense in which they are being used.

It is also essential that the reader should understand that the philosopher's 'public knowledge' does not equate with the idea of social knowledge used here; nor does his 'private knowledge' equate with our usage of the term 'personal knowledge'. As previously defined, in our terminology, social knowledge is distinguished from personal knowledge by the characteristic of availability. The difference between the philosopher's public knowledge and his private knowledge can be seen as being a question of what the knowledge is *about*. Public knowledge is *about* the external world, perceivable by anyone through his senses, and regardless of whether it has been recorded or not. Private knowledge is *about* the inner feelings of the person who knows it, and not perceivable by another person through his senses. The point is a difficult one, which is liable to become confused when the literature from different fields is examined, because of different uses of terminology by different writers. In particular, Ziman uses the term 'Public Knowledge' with a meaning which resembles the sense in which we use 'social knowledge'; and Popper uses the term 'objective knowledge' in a similar way. We can say, however, that the reader must have four different concepts for the terms public knowledge, private knowledge, social knowledge and personal knowledge. When these terms are used in this book, public and private knowledge refer to the philosopher's usage, and social and personal knowledge are used with the meanings ascribed to them in chapter 3. When reference is made to Ziman's concept of Public Knowledge, it will be distinguished by using initial capital letters.

If the distinctions are clear to him, the reader will be in a position to understand that public knowledge can remain personal knowledge. As an example, under my front lawn there is a trench full of builder's rubble. This is personal knowledge because (until now) it has not been recorded; it is public knowledge because it can be perceived by the senses, and anyone who digs up the lawn will certainly perceive it: at certain points, his spade will not get very far. It is, perhaps, rather more difficult to appreciate that private knowledge can be a source of ('source of inspiration for' is a rather better expression) social knowledge. This is because writers and other creative artists can and do attempt to create documents which portray, as far as their abilities allow, the emotions which they themselves feel, or which they imagine their characters may or would have felt. As an obvious example, one might claim that the plays of Shakespeare are great works of art, not because of their account of historical events, but because they are very successful attempts to show in words and actions how the characters who took part in these events must have felt: or, in other words, what their private knowledge may have been like at the time of the events.

Conclusions

What conclusions can be drawn from this very brief account of what philosophy has to tell us about the nature of knowledge? The first point is, perhaps, that there is no conclusion, and no easy answer to the problem of the nature of knowledge. Philosophers have not been able to produce a definition of knowledge which satisfies their rules, and on which they all agree. They have, however, introduced into their discussions, ideas and problems which have been taken up by other branches of learning; by science in general, and by psychology in particular in the case of the nature of knowledge. We have already had occasion to refer to this.

The reader should also remember that the philosophy which we have discussed in this chapter, is concerned almost exclusively with the knowledge of the individual, with what we have called personal knowledge; thus, the statement on which much of the discussion was based was 'I know' and not 'We (as a society) know' (see also p 78). Increasingly, however, attention is being turned towards the philosophical examination of what we have called social knowledge. Much of the concern is with the nature of scientific knowledge in particular, and we shall, in fact, examine philosophical ideas about social knowledge in our discussion of scientific knowledge and its philosophy.

We have also examined philosophical ideas about the existence of different sources of knowledge, and these will be re-examined when the question of the possible existence and importance of different kinds of knowledge, apart from the distinction between social and personal knowledge, is discussed.

It should be noted that all these points, apart from the first, are not proper conclusions, but indications of where we go from here. This, perhaps, is a useful function of philosophy: to consider what are the right sorts of questions to ask; these questions may be taken as starting points for other methods of investigation.

Finally we might note that epistemology is not the only branch of philosophy, and that the branch known as logic has much to offer in relation to the theory of classification and information retrieval (3).

NOTES AND REFERENCES

1 The works consulted in compiling this chapter were, principally, Ayer (1956) and Chisholm (1966). Some of the ideas came from hearing on BBC Radio a series of talks which have since been published (Magee 1971)). For Popper, see Popper (1965) (1972) and Magee (1973).

2 Hoffmann (1970). See also chapter 5, note 25.

3 Stebbing (1952) ch 6 is a good source.

Chapter 5

PSYCHOLOGY AND KNOWLEDGE

INTRODUCTION: We continue our examination of the nature of knowledge by considering what we can learn from psychology. There are numerous different definitions of the term: a full discussion of them would be the subject of an entire book. Two which are useful for us are firstly, that psychology is the science concerned with human knowledge; and secondly, it is the science of mental life.

These definitions indicate two features of psychology. One is that psychology is a science and its practitioners use scientific methods. These methods are discussed fairly fully in chapter 6, but for the moment, it need only be said that psychologists conduct experiments and make observations, and from these draw inferences or conclusions. Secondly, psychology is about human behaviour—why and how people act as they do. It is concerned with mental processes such as thinking and learning, and with mental states such as happiness (1). One aspect of human mental behaviour is communication. Indeed, the human abili⁺y to communicate has been advanced by some writers as that which makes us human as distinct from animal, although there is now evidence that this is not so, and that chimpanzees, at least, have the same kind of communication abilities as humans (2). Psychology is a source of information not only about the nature of knowledge, but also about how it is communicated. It is, therefore, of particular interest to librarians.

It is related to and overlaps with a number of other topics, and is useful when considered in relation to them. Until the end of the nineteenth century, psychology was considered to be a branch of philosophy. As a philosophical study, it was concerned with problems such as the nature of memory. It was developed as a science when philosophical discussion began to be replaced by a scientific approach to discovering the answers to these questions and eventually its scope was enlarged to include other aspects of human behaviour (3). This change in status is used as an example later.

41

Psychology is very largely concerned with the individual; social psychology, however, is concerned with groups and their behaviour. Our concern in this chapter is with the individual and his personal knowledge, and we leave consideration of social psychology, and what it has to teach us about the nature of social knowledge, to chapter 7. (Obviously at certain points in this chapter the group's effect on the individual has to be considered).

One definition of psychology suggests that it is concerned with the mind. The notion of 'mind' is, according to some writers, a highly unscientific idea, which reflects only the philosophical origins of the subject (4). We cannot properly define the term 'mind', but we can define the term 'brain', and they suggest that this is what should be investigated; *eg,* by considering what changes take place in the brain when something is learnt, and how the brain stores knowledge. The science which is concerned with the functioning of the brain is called neurophysiology. Between it and psychology there is no clear boundary; and there are physiological psychologists who concern themselves with such things as the physiological processes involved in perception, particularly in vision. On the other hand some psychologists, notably in what is called the stimulus-response (S-R) school, have taken the view that we cannot understand the physiological processes in the brain. Therefore, they interested themselves only in the relations between what goes into the mind (or brain), *ie* the stimulus, and what happens as a result (the response). What happens between the stimulus and the response was to them unimportant; it happens, as it were, in a sealed box whose inner workings cannot be understood. At the end of the chapter we discuss neurophysiology very briefly.

Psychology is the conduct of scientific investigation into the phenomena of human behaviour, and particularly of 'normal' behaviour. It is distinct from psychiatry, whose concern is the alleviation or cure of 'sick' (abnormal) human behaviour and states. There is of course much interchanging of ideas between psychology and psychiatry.

Psychology and knowledge
It is possible to distinguish five processes in relation to knowledge:
learning—acquiring knowledge which someone else knows;
creating—acquiring knowledge which no one else knows;
retaining—remembering, knowing;
communicating;
using.
The first four of these may be called perceptual-cognitive processes. It may be noted that for the purposes of psychology it is not always possible

or necessary to distinguish between the first two—they are both processes whereby an individual acquires knowledge; and whether or not some other individual has previously acquired that knowledge is irrelevant so far as the study of the process is concerned. There is no essential difference in the mental process of the hotel guest who discovers that the water in the hot tap is not merely hot, it is scalding (which may be well known to the other guests and the hotel staff); and the process in the mind of the engineer who discovers that the thermostat is stuck, something no one else knew; and the scientist who makes a discovery may have used the same mental process as both of them. However some psychologists do concern themselves particularly with the second of the five processes, with the psychology of creativity (5). We can now consider a number of ideas which are fairly basic to the processes of learning and creating, remembering, and communicating.

Concepts

The reader is asked to look at the diagram in figure 1, which represents a two-volume dictionary in which the first entry is 'a' and the last word is 'zythum'. Each of the volumes is two inches thick, and the covers of the volume are 1/8 inch thick. Now think of a bookworm. Imagine that the bookworm starts at 'a' and eats its way through to 'zythum'. How far will it have travelled?

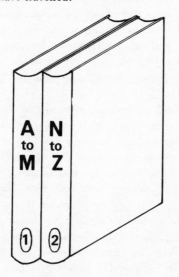

Figure 1:
A two-volume
dictionary
on a shelf.

The answer to the problem is 1/4 inch—through the front cover of volume 1 and through the back cover of volume 2. The answer however is not important; what matters is that when you read the words 'dictionary', 'volume', 'inches', and 'bookworm' you thought of something; what you thought of was your *concept* relating to the word. You may, when you read the word 'dictionary', have thought of an alphabetically arranged list of words with definitions or explanations of them—that (or whatever you thought of) was the concept which you associate with the word 'dictionary'. Some other points may be demonstrated by this example. Firstly, when you saw the word 'zythum', it is likely that you were unable to think of anything, except that it was an unusual word whose meaning you did not know—*ie* you had *no concept* to associate with the word. In fact, zythum is a kind of beer. *You now have a concept to which the word relates.* You will not find zythum in any pub or bar. My dictionary says that it was brewed (and presumably drunk) by the ancient Egyptians. *You now have a better concept* associated with the word; you have learnt something.

The second point is illustrated by the two concepts which you may well associate with the word 'bookworm': a bookworm is either an avid reader or else a pest which makes holes in books. Thirdly, and conversely, the word 'volume' may mean the same to you as the word 'book'. Thus there is no one-to-one relationship between concepts and words—a word may well invoke more than one concept, and there may be more than one word to associate with any one concept. We return to this point later.

Finally, if I were able to show you one of the things illustrated in figure 1, you might well think of something—which is (presumably) your concept of a book (or perhaps of a volume or dictionary). Concepts can be aroused or invoked—stimulated—not only by words, but also by actions or physical objects. In fact, they can be stimulated by or through any of the senses.

There are numerous different definitions of concepts. They can be regarded as the 'vehicles of thought'—what we think with. Another definition is that a concept is a 'label of a set of things with something in common'. For example our concept of 'book' is the label which our mind uses for objects which have in common the characteristics of books. Such definitions may imply that concepts are, as it were, 'things'. Other definitions of concepts imply that they are processes. One of these is that a concept is an 'implied process which enables us to classify objects'. For example, if I hold up a book in front of you, you would recognize that the object being shown to you was a book. This definition says that from our ability to recognize individual objects as belonging to particular categories, we can infer that a process of classification takes place when we do so—the term concept may be used to refer to this process.

Another definition of a concept, which perhaps expands on this idea, is that it is a 'kind of selective subsystem in the mental organisation of a person which links previous experience and current states with stimuli'. A person has seen and read numerous books in the past—this is his previous experience of them. As a result, he has ideas about what books are like—these form the current state of his mind in relation to books. When he sees another one (the stimulus) he links this with his ideas of books which are based on his previous experience of them. In the definition, the concept is this process of linking or association (6).

We may note the extent to which these definitions incorporate the idea of classification. In one definition the word classification itself was used. In the others, the idea of classification is suggested by the ideas of labelling, of sets of things and of selection. All of these have the implication of distinguishing some things from other things, and classification (in one sense) is merely a term used instead of 'distinguishing' (7).

Many psychologists point to the fact that it has not, so far, been possible to prove the existence of concepts (for example by finding physiological effects which can be ascribed to their acquisition (see also p 57-58)) and they argue that we ought not to discuss concepts as though they are real, because it is a highly unscientific procedure to discuss phenomena for whose reality there is no scientific evidence. This viewpoint is the same as that discussed earlier in relation to the idea of 'mind' (8). Many books on general psychology do not therefore mention concepts. Nevertheless the 'concept of concepts' is considered in many books on the psychology of learning, and it is difficult to see how it would be possible to consider the nature of human knowledge and learning without having resort to the discussion of them. Some writers avoid the term itself, but use other expressions, such as 'mental image', to refer to what is fundamentally the notion of concepts. Another term used is 'schema' (plural *schemata*), though this is conveniently used not for individual concepts, but for the total pattern of relationships between all the concepts a person has—his total 'mental image', or his entire collection of knowledge, ideas and opinions (9).

The role of concepts
Assuming that concepts exist, further appreciation of their nature can be gained by examining their roles or functions—what they are used for, and how (10). To illustrate this, we can take the example of Mr Bloggs, who is a regular traveller by bus to various destinations.

1 Concepts relate causes and effects.

Sometime during his childhood, Mr Bloggs will have acquired the concept that the faster an object moves towards a certain point, the sooner that point will be reached. Mr Bloggs will have used this concept to form another one: fast buses reach their destination sooner than slow ones.

2 Concepts enable action to be taken or avoided.

If Mr Bloggs has this concept about fast buses, it (in conjunction with another concept), will enable him to take the action of getting on those buses which will get him to his destination soonest, and to avoid the action of getting on those buses which will take longer (or *vice versa*, if he so wishes).

3 Concepts enable us to identify things.

Probably the buses have numbers which identify their routes. If Mr Bloggs has this concept, and also concepts of which numbers are used for the fast buses, (this is the additional concept mentioned previously), then he will be able to identify the fast buses. This situation would still leave Mr Bloggs with a problem—that of remembering which are the numbers of the fast buses. The numbers of the fast buses are too many and too random to be remembered easily. Fortunately the bus companies appreciate this, and so prefix the numbers for their fast (or express) buses with the letter X. This does two things for Mr Bloggs.

4 Concepts reduce the complexity of the environment.

Mr Bloggs's life is made simpler by the fact that he no longer has to remember a long list of random numbers representing fast buses; he need only remember the special feature which identifies them.

5 Concepts reduce the need for constant learning.

If Mr Bloggs is in a strange place and wishes to use a fast bus, there is no need for him to learn their numbers; he need only use the concept which he already has (of the significance of X) to allow him to find the fast ones.

Learning

Learning may be conveniently described as that part of human behaviour concerned with the acquisition of knowledge (or concepts) (11). Because of the importance of the learning process in relation to the improvement of educational methods, much effort has been expended by psychologists on its study. Our present interest lies in the fact that it may enable us to gain an insight into the nature of knowledge; but we may also note that much of the use made of libraries is for learning, so that the topic has perhaps a double relevance for librarians.

The learning process may be considered as involving three stages: sensation, perception, and conceptualisation, or concept formation. For the purpose of illustration, imagine a boy with a bucket of water with ice in the water. When the boy puts his hand in the bucket, he senses something—he undergoes a sensation. Sensation is difficult to define. (Indeed some writers say that it cannot be defined and should not be regarded as a separate stage.) It may, however, be thought of as equivalent to stimulation in the way in which that term was used in the earlier example about books, or perhaps it is to be considered as 'becoming aware'. It might also be thought of as the stage at which our hero says 'ouch' (which occurs before he realises why he did so). The next stage, perception, follows instantaneously, and is the part of the process in which he identifies what the sensation is—that his hand is unpleasantly cold. Similarly he might perceive (visually) that there is water in the bucket, and/or that there is something in the water. The things which are perceived are referred to as 'percepts'. The third stage, conceptualisation, is not usually instantaneous, and may require repeated experiences of the simultaneous occurrence of the same set of percepts. In this example, the boy might, after sufficient experience of putting his hand into buckets of water with ice in them, form the concept that the 'something' in the water has the effect of making it unpleasantly cold.

Perception and conceptualisation are interdependent processes (12). We cannot perceive something unless we have a concept of that thing, and we cannot form concepts of things unless we have the ability to perceive their constituents or properties. (The same point was made in the previous chapter, in the context that knowledge always depends on existing knowledge; the following example was also used there). We cannot see (seeing is, of course, one form of perception) a cow unless we have a concept of a cow—a largish animal with four legs, a head, and udders. Conversely, we cannot form the concept of a cow unless (among other things) we are able to perceive largish four-legged animals with udders. This need for perception is sometimes illustrated by a story of blind men who were taken to examine an elephant (13). Each was given a different part to feel. The man who held a leg thought it was a tree trunk; the man who held the ear thought he had hold of a thick piece of cloth. One man felt the elephant's tail and immediately dropped it and ran away, because he thought he had been given a snake to hold. The man put on its back thought he was on a large stone. None of them was able to perceive all the features of the elephant simultaneously and therefore, they were not able to form the concept of an elephant.

Conceptualisation: the formation of concepts

Conceptualisation is not merely the third stage in learning, it is, more importantly, what makes learning different from other forms of behaviour. Our concept of the room in which we are accustomed to eat will include the concept that there is a table on which we put our plates. If we go into the room and the table is there, we perceive it, but we do not learn anything. because in this case the *per*cept does not require that our *con*cept of the room be changed. If, however, the table were not there, it would be necessary to change our concept of the room; we should learn something. The importance of conceptualisation is underlined by the fact that in many cases, when reference is made to the psychology of learning, it is more precisely the formation of concepts which is being considered.

There is no general consensus on the detail of what goes on in the process of concept formation. It has been suggested that two stages are involved— discrimination, and grouping; and that these are further dependent on the ability to abstract and generalise (14). A young child may, for example, have a concept of 'animals'. Gradually he will *abstract* certain qualities from the animals which he sees, hears, *etc* (which he perceives). He will become able to use these qualities to distinguish or *discriminate* between different animals. He will recognise that there are not just animals but that there are animals of different kinds. He may notice, for example, that different animals make different sounds; some of them mew, while others bark. Eventually he may begin to *generalise*—to recognise that lots of animals mew, and perhaps that the quality of mewing is associated with other qualities, such as the ability to climb and jump. On this basis he will begin to *group* together those animals which mew and climb and jump and which are rather smaller than most other animals. When he has done this, he has formed the concept of a cat.

Attention should perhaps be drawn to the fact that discrimination and grouping are processes which define classification: classification can be quite comprehensively described as discrimination between unlike objects and the grouping of like objects. It may also be noted that classification (and grouping) are both particular forms or methods of organisation. We will return to both of these points later.

It should be noted that the description given of the way in which a child uses the processes of abstraction/discrimination and generalisation/ grouping is almost certainly an oversimplification. It assumes that the child thinks or reasons in the same way as an adult, and that there is an orderly sequence involved; whereas it is much more likely that all the processes occur simultaneously in a haphazard manner. Also, of course,

48

words are not necessarily involved. An obvious piece of evidence for this is a small child wanting something and adults finding out what it is by trial and error. If he knows what he wants, only that will satisfy the child. He may not have a word for it but he quite clearly has a concept of it.

The same thing can, of course, happen in adulthood. The reader may have had the experience of seeing something which it would be useful to him to have, but of not having the opportunity of finding out its name. He then has a concept of what he wants, without having a word by which to describe it—which makes asking for the desired object in shops rather difficult.

Factors affecting knowledge

A number of different factors have been found to affect the processes of perception and conceptualisation (15). As these are, as described, the processes by which knowledge is acquired, they are factors which may be said to affect our knowledge.

Previous experience

Our knowledge depends on previous experience. If we have had the opportunity to experience certain things, we have had the opportunity to form concepts of them; if we have not had the experience, we will not have had the opportunity to form the concepts. In this connection, hearing or reading someone else's description of his experience may be regarded as vicarious experience, but nevertheless it is still experience. (Moreover, in this case our knowledge or concept may be affected by the actual experience of hearing or reading the account given by the speaker or author. If, for example, it is told in a sombre voice, our concept may include the notion of the gravity of the situation: but if it is told with a smile, we may form the concept that the experience is a source of amusement.)

To exemplify the dependence of concepts on experience, visualise the following four things: a caterpillar, a breadcrumb, a pin and a dead fly (16). These seem to adults to have nothing in common which would allow us to group them together. If we consider the experience of a very young child, however, we can recognise that they might well have a common attribute within that experience—they are all things which a mother might pick up from the floor and put in a wastebin. The reason for the choice of example is, incidentally, that a child has been observed to use the same name for all four objects, which suggests that at the time he had the same concept for all of them.

49

This dependence on experience relates not only to conceptualisation—which probably depends on experience over comparatively long periods of time—it also applies to our perception, which is dependent on, or relative to, our immediate past experience (17). If we go into our houses on cold nights, the hall of the house is likely to feel warm: we will perceive it as warm. If, thereafter, we sit in front of the fire for some time, and then leave the room in which we have been sitting and go into the hall, our percept of the hall on that occasion will be that it is cold. The idea is illustrated in figure 2: how we interpret the central part depends on whether we look at the horizontal row, the vertical column, or both.

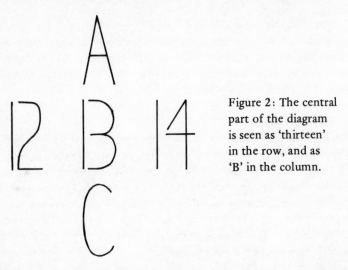

Figure 2: The central part of the diagram is seen as 'thirteen' in the row, and as 'B' in the column.

Time

The passage of time affects our concepts: they change with time. This could be looked upon as a result of the previous point; because, as time passes, the individual gains more and different experiences. Thus, the child in the earlier example may have the experience, or perceive, that the caterpillar moves, that the pin is sharp, and that while he is allowed to eat a breadcrumb which is on a table, his mother will not allow him to consume a dead fly. Fairly detailed observations have been made of the way in which a child's experiences have affected the concepts he appears to have.

The concepts of adults also change with time, although in their case there is evidence that they change more slowly (one possible reason, among others, being that as the years pass, they have fewer new experiences)

50

The evidence also shows that, consciously or subconsciously, adults tend to resist changing their concepts, as witness the wife who in an altercation with her husband said, 'Don't bother me with the facts—I know what I believe.' The scientific evidence is that adults are much more receptive to facts or ideas which tend to strengthen or confirm their existing concepts, than they are to those facts which would require them to alter them. Other evidence suggests that in children the process is truly one of *forming* new concepts, while in adults the process is much more one of changing existing concepts. The knowledge of adults does not so much increase as change (18).

'Preconception'

Perhaps connected with the idea that adults tend to accept only the notions which confirm what they already believe, is that our perceptions tend to be affected by what we think we ought to perceive (19). This relates to the Gestalt school of psychology, which puts forward the idea that we tend to perceive whole patterns which are familiar to us, and if, in fact, what we perceive only nearly matches the standard pattern, then we automatically compensate for whatever is different from the pattern. Figure 2 also serves as illustration of this. When we perceive the central part of the diagram as the letter 'B', we automatically ignore the fact that there are gaps between the straight vertical line and the ends of the curves. Compare also the figure 4 in the diagram.

Reverting to the example of the bucket of water with ice in it: an adult who perceived that the bucket contained cold water, and that there were transparent solid blocks floating in it, would probably not perceive simply transparent solid blocks, but rather blocks of ice; because in view of the coldness of the water, this is what he would expect them to be. They might, however, be blocks of perspex. This has great humorous potential. On a television show, there was a sequence which showed a young lady lying in bed in what appeared to be a very sinister castle. The bedroom door creaked slowly open to reveal the shadow of a hand holding a long pointed object—a dagger? When the hand came into the light, the object turned out to be an oilcan with a long spout, which was then used to oil the creaking hinges of the door.

Instances of perception depending on what is thought ought to be perceived are recorded in the history of the sciences, even though it is an essential part of scientific method that precautions are taken to ensure not only that this does not, but cannot happen (the idea of objectivity). A well known and highly respected astronomer, van Maanen, early in this century made some photographic observations and then carried out measurements on the photographs with special equipment. The results, as he recorded and published them, were a major part of the evidence for a theory that was widely held to be correct for the next twenty or thirty years.

Gradually, however, the accumulated weight of other evidence was in favour of an alternative theory, until eventually only the observations of van Maanen (who in the intervening years had died) remained to support the original theory and refute its alternatives. Eventually, three astronomers procured his photographs and equipment and repeated his measurements, using exactly the method he had described. Their results were quite different from van Maanen's, and supported the new alternative theory. They found no evidence to suggest that van Maanen had consciously tried to falsify his results, or any to suggest that he had anything at all to gain from doing so. The only conclusion which can be drawn is that when he made his measurements he knew what he would expect to find according to the then prevalent theory, and this alone was enough to ensure that in spite of all his attempts to be objective, he found it.

Other similar instances are the canals of Mars; and the recent discovery of pulsars, in which the training of the astronomers involved led them to think—only half-humorously—of 'little green men'. Only afterwards did they realise that they were observing radiation of an unusual kind from a hitherto unknown and unsuspected kind of astronomical body—the pulsars (20).

False perception

A feature of perception is that it may be false. There are several psychological (and social) factors which produce this effect, but they need not be discussed here. Optical illusions are an obvious example (21): one which is well known is reproduced in figure 3. We may say that seeing is not, or ought not always to be, believing—our senses can mislead us.

Differences in logical thought

Differences in logical thought can result in different concepts being developed from the percepts derived from the same objects (16). This factor cannot, perhaps, be separated completely from the factor (or influence) of previous experience; but it has been observed that as children develop, so too does their capacity for logical thought—they learn to think in new, different, ways. Given a collection of carpenter's tools to

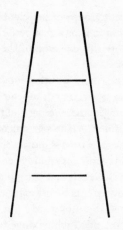

Figure 3:
Which
horizontal
line is
longest?

arrange, for instance, a young child may group them according to the colour of the handles, while an older child, or an adult, is more likely to group them by purpose into hammers, screwdrivers, chisels, etc. The caterpillar, breadcrumb, pin and dead fly example may also be an illustration of this point.

Social factors

The final factor affecting our knowledge is the way social factors affect our perception. This point will be discussed more fully in chapter 7, but one example can be given here (22). South Africans, whose social background is very strongly influenced by the sharp distinction made in their country between the black and white races, tend not to recognise that there are intermediate grey shades. Would a South African shown the middle patch in figure 4 be likely to say that it is black (or white), whereas someone from another country is likely to say that it is grey?

Figure 4:
How many
different shades
can you see?

Concepts, words and meanings

Earlier, the point was made that there is no one-to-one correspondence between words and concepts: there are two concepts at least which are likely to be associated with the word 'bookworm'. Not only do words stimulate different concepts for different individuals, and for the same individual at different times according to circumstances, they will also invoke different concepts in different groups of people; as, for example, the word 'volume' to a group of librarians or a group of chemists. The purpose of what follows is to explore this question of the relationship between words and their meanings.

One of the definitions given of concepts was that they are 'labels of sets of things which have something in common', to which might be added the fact that they are used in learning, remembering and thinking. Words (most of them) can be similarly defined as labels of sets of things which have something in common: the use of words is, however, in communication. We have just recalled that nevertheless there is no direct and unvarying relationship between words as labels and concepts as labels. The writer usually demonstrates this to students by asking them to write six words which they associate with one stimulus word. For example, on one occasion the stimulus word was 'cows', which drew from nearly all students such expected responses as 'fields' and 'butter'. It also drew forth three unexpected responses—'trains', 'Littlehampton' and 'Pink Floyd'—from individual students who, respectively, lived in the centre of a city and had only ever seen cows during railway journeys; had as a young child been chased by cows near Littlehampton; and who had just bought a pop group record on the sleeve of which there appeared a cow.

We may express the idea that the concepts associated with words are different for different people, by saying that words have different meanings for different people: we might also say that the meaning a word has for an individual is the concepts that he associates with the sight or sound of the word (23). One reason for the different meanings that different words have for different individuals is that there are two different kinds of meaning—denotation and connotation (24).

Denotation

The denotation of a word is the thing which it represents or refers to. In the case of a word which refers to a tangible object, we can give its definition by pointing to the thing and saying 'This is a . . .', or 'That is a . . .'. The object pointed to is technically called the *referent*. In the case of intangible referents, it is more difficult to define the denotations of the words used. We have already pointed out that 'philosophy' has different meanings—different denotations—in different parts of the world. Other examples are goodness and badness, or steepness and height. In the case of the latter two, the denotations are likely to be quite different for someone who lives in the English Fenlands or the American wheatlands, as compared with someone who lives in the Welsh mountains, or in the Rockies. Generally, though, for people with the same cultural and environmental background, words have, and must have, the same denotation for all of them; otherwise communication would be impossible and words have no useful purpose. Unless all my readers share the denotation which I have for 'cat', the illustration given earlier will be of little use.

Connotation

By contrast, the connotation of a word is highly individual and personal. The reader may be a cat lover, in which case his connotation of 'cat' may include the notion of friendliness, warmth, purring and the particular example of the cat at home. The writer is not a cat lover, and his connotation of 'cat' includes smelliness and screeching at night. These examples serve to show that connotation is related to how we feel about things, the ways in which we are emotionally affected by them. This consideration gives rise to the use of the term 'affective' for connotative knowledge (see below). We can define the connotation of a word as the ideas and qualities or concepts which an individual associates with it, as opposed to and exclusive of, the ideas and qualities which everybody, *ie* society, associates with it.

Comments on denotation and connotation

Appropriately enough, if the reader consults other books on this point, he will find that other writers use different terms for the concepts we have named denotation and connotation (25). He will find too that these terms are also used in the contexts of (philosophical) epistemology and of the theory of classification; but there they have different meanings (although their meanings in those contexts can be shown to have a connection with their meanings in the present context). These other terms and their relationships are shown in table 1. It should be noted that, although the various uses of the terms can all be traced back to origins in philosophy, the uses now made of them are by no means consistent and can be confusing when different writers are consulted. The warning given in the previous chapter is worth repeating: always check the definitions of these terms given by the writers who use them.

The idea that concepts vary or change with time has already been discussed. It follows, therefore, that denotations and connotations also vary with time. As we learn the meaning of a word, the denotation which we give it corresponds more and more closely to the denotation given to it by members of the society of which we are part—our home

DENOTATION/denotative	CONNOTATION/connotative
informative	affective
extension/extensional	intension/intensional
objective	subjective
public	private

Table 1

when we are children, and later in life, the working community to which
we belong. Our original denotation of 'table' may be the place at which
we eat; later, it may be that it is a place at which we eat, work and play
games upon; and then, more generally, a flat surface standing on legs.
Denotations, of course, also change with time among a society. A nice
example of this is the word 'nice' itself, which used to mean 'exact', but
now more usually means 'good', 'pleasant'. (The reason for this particular
change is shown by examining the first use of the word 'nice' in the previous sentence, for which the words 'exact' and 'good' could both be
substituted in that context). Connotations also change, perhaps more
rapidly than denotations. We may have the cat-lovers' connotations of
'cat', but if one scratches and bites us, then our connotations are likely
to be affected, if not changed completely.

More generally, it can be claimed that meaning changes with *context*
(of which time is but one aspect) *ie* the place where it is used, the persons
among whom it is used, and its relationship to other words in the same
context. Thus 'volume' has a meaning in librarianship which is determined
by its relationship to the term 'book' (and the term 'work'); whereas in
chemistry, its meaning is determined by its relationship with 'density'
and 'pressure'.

Memory, knowledge and organisation
In discussing concept formation we introduced the ideas of discrimination and grouping, and we mentioned that these are equivalent to the idea
of classification, which in turn is a form or method of organisation. We
might have claimed that learning is, or involves, a process of classification
and organisation. We now want to present some evidence that memory,
or the retention of knowledge, also seems to depend on the possibility
or facility of organisation, and indeed more specifically of classification
(26).

Quite briefly, the evidence is that if a person is asked to remember
names of (say) animals, he will try to do so by remembering them in

groups. Regardless of the number of animals he would use perhaps five, six, or seven groups (in any case almost certainly not more than nine). He might, for example, group the animals into domestic, wild, farm, and foreign animals, and birds. If any of the groups contained more than between five to nine examples it would be split into sub-groups; foreign animals for example might be subarranged into geographically based sub-groups. Experiments have shown that when people do this, their ability to recall the animals (or whatever) from memory is greater than if they are told not to do so; or if they are presented with the animals in groups not of their own devising. In another set of experiments it was found that the abilities of mentally-retarded people to remember could be increased by suggesting to them that they attempt to group things which they needed to remember (27).

Conclusions: evidence as to the properties of knowledge

The literature of psychology has much to offer anyone who wishes to find ideas as to what the nature of knowledge might be. It suggests that organisation is essential to knowledge: we learn by organising what we perceive, and we remember because we organise, or have organised, our store of knowledge. Without this organisation, our ability to learn and remember would be seriously impaired, or even destroyed. It also suggests the nature of the organisation, namely hierarchical classification. Further, if we are willing to accept that thought processes are themselves methods of organisation, inasmuch as they involve creating relations between different concepts, then we may say that the organisation which we use determines what we know.

What we know depends on what we have experienced (either directly or vicariously). Because of the dependence on direct experience, our knowledge is determined at least in part by our social environment, because it determines what experience we may have. We tend to prefer to learn those things which confirm what we already know or believe: our knowledge is perhaps conservative rather than radical. Last, but not least, not all of what we know, or at least all that we perceive, is necessarily true: our own senses may deceive us.

The brain and the hologram

At the beginning of this chapter we described what neurophysiology is. On examination of the literature, it appears that neurophysiology is a long way from being able to suggest any generally acceptable theory as to what knowledge consists of, or as to how a brain whose owner knows something is different from the brain of someone who does not know it (28). There are, however, a number of hypotheses, one of which is relevant to our study, although the reader may feel that it takes us near to the realm of science fiction.

It is reasonable to suppose that when an individual learns something, some change takes place in his brain. In the jargon of those who are concerned with these matters, we might reasonably expect that when something is learnt, a 'memory trace' or 'engram' will be deposited in the brain. An engram may be considered as the change introduced in the brain when a concept is acquired. It is also reasonable to suppose that if the part of the brain containing the engram were surgically removed, then the engram relating to that particular memory would be destroyed (29). This reasoning is reinforced by knowledge of the relationship between the parts of the brain which control the movements of our limbs, hands, mouth, *etc*, and by the knowledge of the effects of brain damage on the control exercised by the brain.

A whole series of experiments have been conducted on animals on the basis of this reasoning. By teaching them such things as how to obtain food, and then performing neurosurgery on them, it was hoped to be able to discover the part of the brain in which the associated engram was deposited. The experiments have proved totally unsuccessful. Even the removal in some cases of large portions of the brains of the animals involved failed to destroy the engram: after the surgery the animals were still able to remember what they had to do to obtain food. This has led to the hypothesis that perhaps the engram, instead of being deposited in one specific part of the brain, is somehow diffused throughout the brain (so that whatever remained of the brain after the surgery still contained the memory trace) (30).

The hologram also has this property. In making a hologram, the 'coherent' light produced by a laser is used. The diffusion of information stored in holograms is demonstrated in the following way. Imagine an ordinary rectangular photograph, with a diamond, a club, a spade and a heart in each corner. If this were cut into four pieces, one piece would have a diamond on it, another would show a club, and so on. If however the same image were stored in a hologram, the same cutting operation would result in four small holograms, each of which would have all four suits represented on it; their images would be visible when the holograms were illuminated by coherent light.

Holograms also share with the brain the property of being able to store tremendous amounts of information—a rough calculation once suggested that the amount of information which might be stored in a single cubic centimetre of hologram would, if it were to be typed out, take the services of one hundred typists for one thousand years. The suggestion has been made, on the basis of these similarities, that the brain and the hologram are similar in the way in which they store information.

The interest in this stems from the fact that although many people would like to store the world's entire collection of social knowledge in computers at the present time, their storage capacity is not large enough. One of the potential pieces of technology which may eventually be used to overcome this problem is a hologram (31). If this were to come about, it would be used for storing what we have termed 'social knowledge', and in this way we might find that the methods used for storing social knowledge are the same as those used for storing personal knowledge in our brains.

NOTES AND REFERENCES

1 Of the numerous textbooks on psychology and on the psychology of learning, Munn (1966), Lindsay (1972) and Gazzaniga (1973) are all useful, and Hilgard (1971) has been recommended by students. These books all have good annotated bibliographies.

2 On the uniqueness of human communication, see Hebb (1972), p 255-261, Penland (1971) and Lyons (1970). On the animal experiments and the conclusions see Thorpe (1975) p 283-301 and Premack (1972).

3 On the history of psychology, Bruno (1972) is brief, while Murphy (1972) is a standard work. There is also a Penguin publication of a work by Thompson (1968).

4 The word is often not found in the indexes of textbooks.

5 For example, Guilford (1968), Bruner (1956): the latter is something of a classic. More philosophical discussions are also contained in Koestler (1966) and Stent (1972).

6 For definitions see Klausmeier (1966) and Asher (1953).

7 For general discussions see Hilgard (1971), Hayakawa (1963) ch 12, Bourne (1971) p 246. For discussions by librarians see Jones (1974) and Langridge (1973).

8 Petyt (1972).

9 Sampson (1971) p 149, Mortensen (1972) p 122, Gazzaniga (1973) p 140.

10 Bruner (1956) p 12-13.

11 Thompson (1959) ch 4. Also: Beard (1969), Gazzaniga (1973) ch 7, P. R. Miller (1969) ch 9, Lindsay (1972) ch 13, Vygotsky (1962) and Werner (1963) p 184 ff.

12 For introductory accounts of perception, see Held (1972).

13 Ornstein (1972) ch 7.

14 Beard (1969) ch 9; and Gazzaniga (1973) ch 7, Lindsay (1972) ch 13.

15 Mortensen (1972) ch 3.

16 Vinacke (1952) p 117, Gazzaniga (1973) p 178-179, Lindsay (1972) p 432.

17 Parry (1967) p 103.

18 Vinacke (1952) p 120.

19 Bourne (1971) p 42.

20 Kuhn (1970) ch 10 (revolutions as changes of world view). For van Maanen see Hetherington (1972).

21 For example, Gregory (1968), (1970), Robinson (1972), Lindsay (1972) ch 1; also Gregory in Held (1972).

22 Mortensen (1972) p 92.

23 For relevant discussion of how different the concepts can be, see Dance (1970) and Minter (1968), which discusses the meanings of 'communication'. See also Carney (1972) p 84 ff.

24 Kemp (1974), Lindgren (1973) p 320 ff, Morris (1946), Rubinstein (1973) p 28, and Vinacke (1952).

25 Hayakawa (1963) p 58 ff and Langridge (1973) discuss some of the terms. See also chapter 4, note 2.

26a The classic paper on 'spans' is Millar (1956) which has been frequently reprinted. The topic is re-examined in the light of later research in Broadbent (in Kennedy (1975) ch 1). See also Johnson-Laird (1974). Harmon (1971) suggests memory spans as the reason for the evolution of new specialisations.

26b For organisation and hierarchy in memory see Mandler (1967) which is a very clear account. See also Hilgard (1971) p 243; Estes (1970) p 134-136, Manis (1966) p 21-26, Pribram (1969a), and Wortmann (1971). There is disagreement between Norman (1969) p 119 and Haslerud (1972) p 102: this is an example of Public Knowledge containing a 'problem' (see chapter 6). Lindsay (1972) ch 10 and 11 are based on linguistic analysis involving cases. For a very recent and relevant account of memory (and a comparison with 'knowledge'), see Restle (1975) ch 11 and 13.

26c Morton (in Kennedy (1975) ch 5) discusses applications to on-line data retrieval systems.

27 Spitz (1966).

28 Hebb (1972) and Luria (1973) are textbooks; Rosenblith (1967) is brief and introductory.

29 Lashley (in Evans (1966)) is a good account by the person chiefly responsible.

30 Pribram (1971) ch 8.

31 . Mezrich (1969) is a brief popular account, Johnson (1970) is a review, Caulfield (1970) ch 13 is a textbook account, while Kock (1972) p 90-91 describes hologram capacity.

Chapter 6

THE PHILOSOPHY OF SCIENCE AND SOCIAL KNOWLEDGE

INTRODUCTION: The purpose of this chapter is the examination of the contribution of the philosophy of science towards an understanding of the nature of social knowledge. The relevance of this subject to social knowledge lies firstly in that it can be argued that scientific knowledge is the model of social knowledge—the kind of knowledge which most clearly demonstrates the properties of social knowledge. Secondly, for science, perhaps more than for any other area of human activity, the existence of social knowledge is essential. These arguments are discussed more fully later in the chapter. We might also point out that there is of course no clear separation between epistemology, as discussed in chapter 4, and certain of the topics discussed here.

It is useful to make clear exactly what is meant by science (1). The aim of science is to increase knowledge of man and of the world in which he lives: what they are made of, and how they work. This definition of science distinguishes it from technology; because the latter, unlike science, is not concerned with knowledge for its own sake. Technology is concerned with discovering and *using* knowledge to produce things which are useful. The things might be a new material or new machinery, or a new process. The typical scientist is not concerned with producing useful things in this sense: what he does is produce knowledge.

It may be said that the aim of the scientist is to know as much as possible: the aim of the technologist is to know as much as is useful. Of course, the technologist may employ the knowledge produced by scientists, in order that he may make things: and the same person may one day be concerned with science as defined here and the next day with technology. Although we shall not discuss the question here, it can usefully be mentioned that the differences between science and technology are relevant as their practitioners tend to have different needs for, and attitudes towards, knowledge.

A traditional view of scientific method

We begin by describing scientific method in a way which is to a certain extent traditional, and which, although somewhat idealised and over-simplified, nevertheless provides a means of explaining some basic ideas and a standard against which to compare an alternative description (2). Generally we have used one simple, hypothetical example, rather than real case histories, because the latter often require too much explanation, and divert attention from the point of view which they are supposed to exemplify. In this view of scientific method there are three main elements:

induction }
deduction } methods of argument

testing: experiment and observation

Very briefly, the method consists of using some particular known or established ideas as a starting point, arguing from those that something is generally the case (induction); arguing further by deduction that there will be a particular consequence of the general case; and then conducting an experiment or test to see whether that consequence corresponds to reality.

Induction and deduction

It is necessary to explain the meaning of the terms induction and deduction fully. Induction is arguing that because something is true in a particular case, then it will also apply more generally. It is argument from the particular to the general. For example:

The Moon is made of green cheese

is a particular statement made about a particular satellite of a particular planet. By using inductive argument we may reach the conclusion that:

All satellites of all planets are made of green cheese.

Such general statements are the starting points for arguments by deduction, which proceeds from them to a particular case. For example, in addition to the general statement given, it could be said that:

Norebo is a satellite of the planet Sunaru

and from the two statements we can deduce that:

Norebo is made of green cheese.

The general statement that satellites are made of green cheese might be an example of a *hypothesis:* the conclusions of inductive arguments used in science often are. Hypotheses may be regarded as the first (or an early) *stage* in scientific method. Here is another example of a hypothesis:

Potato plants which are grown in ashy soil grow better than those which are grown in soil which is not ashy.

This hypothesis might have been arrived at from an observation of a potato plant which did grow exceptionally well and whose roots were in ashy soil. Hypotheses can be regarded as tentative conclusions. They can also be regarded as tentative explanations. For example, the same observation might have led to the tentative explanation that:

That potato plant is growing particularly well, *because* it is growing in ashy soil.

It is important to emphasise the tentative and preliminary nature of hypotheses: they are not statements that something *is* the case, only that it *might* be. Potato plants grown in ashy soil may not *all* grow better than those in soil without ash: it may not be that the cause of the exceptionally good growth was the ashiness in the soil.

The process of deduction represents a further stage in scientific method. Here we must emphasise that the purpose in making the deductions is not merely to reach conclusions, but to reach conclusions which can be tested. It would be useless to deduce that the observed potato plant would not have grown as well had there been no ash in the soil, because the same plant cannot be made to grow a second time. It is, however, useful to reach conclusions about another plant, because the effect of ash on its growth is something which it will be possible to test. It there is no means of testing a hypothesis, *ie* if there is no single argument, or no series of arguments, which can relate it to some testable consequence, a hypothesis will remain a hypothesis—unless testing becomes possible later. Moreover the aim is not to find just *one* testable prediction or consequence of the hypothesis, but many; as many as possible.

Testing

The testing of the predicted consequences, or 'postulates', by experiment and observation is the next stage in the method. There are various ways in which scientific experiments and observations are carried out; but, in the case of our potato plant example, one experiment which could be of considerable usefulness would be to grow (say) 200 potato plants, all of them in identical conditions, except that half (100 plants) would be in ashy soil and the other hundred would be in soil devoid of ash. This second group would be regarded as the 'control' group. If the first group grew better than the control group, this would be evidence for the hypothesis that potato plants grow better in, or because of, ashy soil. We might say that in the traditional philosophy of science, the purpose of testing is to prove a hypothesis.

The final stage in scientific method is the publication of the results: making them available to other potato plant scientists. This aspect, which of course is very important to us, is discussed later.

Before considering alternative accounts or philosophies of scientific method, this traditional description may be used to explain certain other ideas (which are essentially the same in all philosophies). These are the notions of 'data' *versus* 'inferences', of different levels of inference, of simplicity, of objectivity, and the measurement/quantitative/mathematical/statistical/probabilistic aspect.

Data versus inferences

It is important to draw the distinction between 'inferences' which are a form or constituent of knowledge, and 'data' which are the raw material from which knowledge is made. Referring to our potato plant example and the experiment of growing 200 plants which we described, we may note that we could make one or more measurements for each plant: the result of each measurement is called a 'datum'. Being aware of these measurements or data is not of much help to anybody, nor are we much further forward if we were to link them with data derived from plants grown in ashy soil. It is only when the data are used as the basis of, or as evidence for, the *inference* that potato plants grow better in ashy soil, that there is any *real* increase in knowledge. In chapter 5, we referred to the discovery of pulsars. In that case, the data consisted (quite literally) of squiggles on pieces of paper: it was only when somebody drew the inference that these squiggles represented radio waves from a previously unknown celestial body that there was any advance in the science of astronomy. *Data* may be defined as the records of the results of experiments and observations: the measurements made by scientists. Inferences may be defined as the conclusions which have been drawn from the available data. As we have tried to make clear, the inferences are much more important than the data, in the sense that they, rather than the data, are what scientific knowledge consists of. Nevertheless the data are essential, if *scientific* inferences are to be drawn; without the data derived from experiments and observations, scientific knowledge could not be distinguished from philosophical knowledge. Moreover, as we have already stated and as will be emphasised later, the greater the amount of available data, the more probable it is that correct inferences will be drawn (3).

65

Inferences and the organisation of knowledge

The drawing of inferences may, in a very real sense, be regarded as the first stage in the organisation of knowledge. If we think of science as a system, we can say that the input to the system is data (which is why data were referred to earlier as raw material). A number of organisational processes are carried out on these data: they are selected or identified, categorised, and the various categories are related. In our potato plant example, the observation that the original plant was growing in ashy soil is an example of choosing or identifying appropriate data. The scientist observed the above-average growth of the plant and looked for possible causes; he *selected* one thing about the particular plant, in addition to its growth, which made it different from the other plants in his experience.

After the experiment, the resulting data have to be categorised into data relating to the ashiness of the soil and data relating to growth. These data can also be categorised as data relating to the causes and effects respectively, and can therefore be linked in a cause-and-effect relationship. The output from the scientific system is the inferences which are drawn as a result of this process of organisation: *ie* the result is increased or new knowledge. If the reader observes here a parallel with features of our discussion of the formation and uses of concepts (p 48), this is not surprising, for 'drawing inferences' is of course the same thing as 'forming concepts'.

Levels of inference

We have been using the term 'inference'; earlier we used the term 'hypothesis'. The reader will probably have assumed that hypotheses and inferences are the same thing and in this he would be correct. It is useful, however, to be more precise and to say that hypotheses are one of a number of different kinds or levels of inferences. It is possible and useful to distinguish four such levels, each successive level being dependent on an increased amount of available data as compared with the previous level. The four levels are:

speculation
hypothesis
theory
law

These, of course, are not completely distinct, but merge into each other. The first, speculation, hardly merits the name of inference at all, inasmuch as it is based on very little or no data: it is simply the scientist's hunch or or conjecture that such-and-such might be the case. Nevertheless, specu-lations are important because they provide the impetus to examine the existing data, or to conduct experiments to collect new data, to see whether the conjecture might be correct. Two further points may be made about speculation. Firstly, as a mental process, it involves imagina-tion or insight (see however the discussion of Kuhn's idea of scientific revolutions (p 127). Some speculations, those which revolutionise science, require greater imagination than those which are evolved in the course of 'normal' science. A number of writers who argue that science is not a completely different activity from the humanities take this as a basis for their case: they suggest that having the idea or insight to relate two phenomena (or two sets of data), like ashiness of soil and good growth, is very similar to having the idea for the plot of a novel or a play, the theme of a movement in a symphony, or the composition of a painting. (See also chapter 10, *The universe of knowledge*).

Secondly, we may note that scientists are reluctant to record their speculations, simply because of the absence of supporting data (although there are a few published collections). This means that they are not available in published form and that, therefore, they are not part of what we call social knowledge (just as an author's original outline of the plot of his novel is not social knowledge). It should be mentioned that speculations are 'available' by consulting the scientist himself—by telephoning or writing to him; they may also be mentioned in conver-sations between scientists (one important astronomical idea, the 'Urca process' was named after the nightclub where it was first talked about). This discussion of speculations—of tentative ideas—is an important part of 'informal communication' between scientists (and other scholars), and is one of the advantages of that kind of communication (see also p 75-76).

A hypothesis can be regarded as the level of inference at which there is a certain amount of data available, but only a very small amount, insufficient to allow the inference to be regarded as 'proved'.

A theory can be thought of as an inference based on 'sufficient' data. We may note that the sufficiency both of the data themselves, of the amount of data, and also of the reasoning in the inference, is not some-thing which is determined or evaluated by the scientist who finds the data or who originally put forward the hypothesis from which the theory is developed, but is decided by all the other scientists who are competent to make judgements about the matter. These other scientists (in theory, although not always in practice) base their evaluations on the recorded, published description of the reasoning and data put forward in support of the theory. Again it may be emphasised that the more data there are, and the less that the data are open to question, the greater is the likelihood that the theory will be regarded as 'proven' knowledge.

Finally, a scientific 'law' is supported by vast amounts of data, and there will be a complete absence of any data suggesting that it is incorrect. Such laws also have the general characteristic that they are about something very fundamental. Examples are the law of gravity (which is not disproved by the principles of relativity but is incorporated into them), and the three laws of thermodynamics, of which the second, which relates to entropy, is mentioned in our discussion of systems theory.

Inferences and simplicity

There may be more than one possible explanation for any phenomenon or for any collection of data. It is a general principle in the philosophy of science that of any of a number of possible explanations or inferences, that which is simplest is the best, or at least the most likely (4). 'Simplest' here implies the smallest possible number of assumptions, or the least complicated argument. This principle is often referred to as 'Occam's razor'. A good example occurs in the history of astronomy. If the movements of the planets are to be described on the basis that all movement is circular, and that the Earth is the centre of the solar system (the Ptolemaic system), then well over one hundred circles are required to explain the motions of the seven planets. If however the Sun is regarded as the centre, and the planets move in ellipses, then only seven ellipses are needed. This is the modern system: there is now all sorts of evidence for it, but at the time its ideas were proposed by Copernicus and then by Kepler, its comparative simplicity was a very large part of its appeal.

Objectivity

This is a very important part of scientific philosophy, and indeed is sometimes used as the criterion whereby science is distinguished from other intellectual activities. The basic idea has already been discussed (chapter 3), where the differences between public (objective) and private (subjective) knowledge were explained (5). Objective knowledge is knowledge perceived through the senses, and contrasts with the subjective knowledge of the individual's own emotions. It is regarded as essential that both in the process of testing, and in the use of the resulting data to support hypotheses and theories, the scientist takes every precaution to ensure that he does not allow his own subjective feelings and opinions to affect what he does; in particular, of course, he must not allow himself to be influenced by what he thinks to be the 'correct' theory. Thus the potato plant scientist must ensure that his measurements of the growth of the plants are all made by the same method—he must above all not use different methods to measure the growth of the plants grown in ashy soil as compared with those grown in his control group. Moreover, if it were the case that fifty of the plants in ashy soil had died, or had not produced potatoes, this should not be omitted from his discussion of the results. One of the reasons for the evaluation of theories by other competent scientists (see the earlier discussion of theories) is to ensure that this principle of objectivity has been adhered to, and this in turn is why accounts of scientific research contain descriptions of the methods of testing used: these enable the evaluation to be made properly (proper evaluation may involve the repetition of tests by other scientists, and therefore the descriptions must be sufficiently fully described to permit this).

The principle is not always adhered to, and indeed its very realism has been challenged. Scientists have been known to present data in a way which supported their theories, at the same time failing to point out that it would also have been possible to present it in a way which supported the alternative and competing theories. The notion that objectivity implies that individual scientists are disinterested has been examined by Mitroff (5), who suggests very strongly that the scientist, far from being objectively concerned with the search for 'truth' and unconcerned about the fate of his own ideas, is very much concerned with the success and widespread acceptance of his theories as opposed to those of other scientists. This rivalry between individual scientists may, it is suggested, provide some of the impetus for continuing to carry out scientific research.

Quantification

Partly it may be supposed as a consequence of the desire for objectivity, scientists make measurements. They do not content themselves for instance that a particular potato plant is a tall example of its kind: they measure its height and include this datum in the record of their findings. The idea of tallness is of course a subjective one (we mentioned the relative nature of the concepts of height in chapter 5). Moreover if we think about the statement that one plant is taller than another one, it is apparent that this covers the case where one is 1 m high and the other is 1·0001 m high, as well as the case where one plant is 1 m high and the other is 2 m high—there is considerable difference in the significance of these two comparisons.

Because the results of experiments made by scientists are quantities represented by numbers they can make calculations. For example, instead of there being only two qualities of soil in the potato plant example (ashy and non-ashy), several different grades of ashiness might be investigated: mathematical methods might well be applied in relating the ashiness of the soil to the 'goodness' of the growth of the various groups of plants.

Probability and statistics

Science very commonly does not deal in certainties, but in likelihoods or probabilities. Thus, for example, the potato plant theory will not state that *all* plants grown in ashy soil will grow better than *all* plants grown in non-ashy soil: rather it will state that it is probable that they will grow better.

Probability is measured (or quantified) on a scale from zero for absolute impossibility to one for absolute certainty. Thus the probability of a tossed coin landing 'heads' is ·49999... and the probability of it landing 'tails' is the same. The reason for this quantity not being ·5 is the possibility of the coin landing on its edge. This also explains the point that 1·0 or 0·0 do not usually appear in discussions of probabilities, because it is assumed that there is no such thing as absolute 'dead certainty'.

The potato plant theory may, therefore, take the form that there is (say) a ·75 probability that the ashy-soil plants will do better than their non-ashy soil counterparts (because in the original experiment 75 out of 100 did so). It should be noted that it does not say *which* individual plants will grow better. By the same token and using the same estimated probability, if the writer were to drive all of his thirty-six students to jump through the window of the third-floor lecture room, the theory would predict that twenty-seven of them would be killed: it does not say *which* would be the lucky nine who were merely injured. (However, it does say in relation to each individual student that each has one chance in four of survival). Statistics or statistical method is the term used to describe the calculations dealing with the probabilistic aspect of hypotheses and theories, and also with the significance of data, *eg* the different significances of the first and second comparisons referred to in the section on quantification.

Interim comments

A few further comments can be made about this traditional view of the philosophy of science. Firstly, it has a long history, going back at least to Sir Francis Bacon (6), although he would not have included all the elements which we have discussed (notably he was not a proponent of either induction or quantification: his particular contribution was the wedding of experiment and observation to the use of deduction). Secondly, the method as described here is the model which is used to present publications of scientific theories: a hypothesis is stated, existing data reviewed, consequences of the hypothesis are argued, experiments are described, and finally the results of the experiments are compared with the predicted consequences of the hypothesis, and conclusions drawn.

It has, however, been suggested that this philosophy is not as 'logical' as it appears: in particular the suggestion is that induction is not a justifiable method of argument. Sir Karl Popper claims to have found a way of overcoming this difficulty. In addition he has put forward other, related ideas which are relevant to the notion of social knowledge. We shall now examine these, in conjunction, subsequently, with those of John Ziman. There are four main aspects of the discussion: the solution of the problem of induction, the notion of truth and credibility, the importance of records (of social knowledge) in science, and the relationship of the records to knowledge. Another aspect, the cumulative and changing nature of knowledge, is discussed in chapter 9.

One reason for the acclaim which has been accorded to Popper's philosophy ought to be mentioned before it is discussed in detail. It is that many scientists who take an interest in the philosophy of science believe that it represents, more accurately than the 'traditional' philosophy, what actually happens in the conduct of scientific research (6a). This is not however to deny that there have been very strong criticisms of Popper's ideas.

The problem of induction
The problem of induction was first raised by David Hume, and the problem is, therefore, sometimes referred to as Hume's problem (7). Consider the following two inductive arguments, the second of which will be familiar:

1 The Sun rose in the east this morning, and the Sun has always risen in the east;
   therefore, the Sun *will* rise in the east tomorrow morning.
2 This potato plant, grown in ashy soil, has grown well;
   therefore, any potato plant, grown in ashy soil, *will* grow well.

In both of these examples, the conclusion is reached that something 'will' happen in the future. Hume's problem is that the conclusions of inductive arguments always have this element of prediction in them, either explicitly or implicitly. (To say that plants grow well in ashy soil, implies that plants grown in ashy soil in the future will also grow well). In other words they can always be expressed in the form:

A has happened; .

therefore B *will* happen.

Hume argued—and this is the nub of the matter—that the fact that something has happened in the past is no grounds for believing that it will happen in the future. Furthermore, it does not matter how *frequently* that particular something has previously happened, because this does not affect the prediction that it will happen in the future.

Before we consider this problem we can point out that in our 'traditional' philosophy, induction and the use of reasoning generally were described as stages in scientific method. If induction is called into question—if doubts are thrown on its logical validity—then the whole basis of science and its claim that its theories and laws can be regarded as knowledge, are thrown into doubt. In essence, if on these grounds we cannot use inductive argument, then we cannot prove anything.

Falsifiability and testing

The easiest way of discussing the arguments which Popper claims overcome the problem of induction, is to begin by considering the purpose of testing, *ie* of experiment and observation. In our account of the traditional philosophy of science, the aim of testing is to prove or *verify* the hypothesis. Thus the aim of the potato plant scientist when he conducted the experiment of planting 200 plants, half of them in ashy soil and the others in non-ashy soil, was to prove the hypothesis that potato plants grow better in soil with ash in it: it was to verify it.

Popper's approach to the problem of induction is to state that the purpose of testing is *not* to prove or verify a hypothesis, but to disprove or falsify it. We *cannot* prove anything (this is the implication of Hume's problem, or, to put it another way,

Hypotheses are not verifiable.

On the other hand we can, by testing, show that hypotheses are not correct. If, for example, the potato plant experiment did not show that potato plants benefit from growing in ashy soil, the hypothesis would be regarded as disproved or falsified. In other words:

Hypotheses are falsifiable.

Because hypotheses can be shown to be false by testing them, we can therefore claim that:

Hypotheses are testifiable.
This leads us into the next part of Popper's argument.

Truth and credibility

In the discussion of epistemology in relation to personal knowledge (p 36), it was mentioned that Popper considers the criterion which really matters in deciding whether something constitutes knowledge, or not, is whether it is true or not. The question which obviously arises from this consideration is 'What is truth?' Popper suggests that:

Truth is the statement which contains the least error.

How, then do we decide which is the statement which contains the least error? As the answer to that question, Popper suggests that:

Truth is the statement which is most consistent with other statements which are believed to be true.

If a statement is inconsistent with other statements which are believed to be true, then the assumption is that it contains error; the more that it is consistent with other statements, the more likely it is that it is true. (Compare, however, our discussion on probability as a candidate for the 'third statement' differentiating knowledge from true opinion.) We might call the absence of statements with which some hypothesis is inconsistent, the 'absence of negative evidence' (in the sense of evidence to the contrary, or refuting or falsifying evidence). The absence of negative evidence is then a reason for judging a statement to be true, or alternatively, for regarding it as credible.

The need for testing

The absence of negative evidence is not, however, sufficient grounds for believing a statement to be true, for deeming it to be credible. If there is *no* evidence, there can obviously be no negative evidence. If, for example, our potato plant man had produced the idea out of his head (and without the evidence of his observation of the single potato plant which we mentioned originally) it would have been, as earlier described, a speculation. There would be no negative evidence against this speculation, but this would be because, and only because, there was no evidence of any sort.

Credibility therefore depends on the absence of negative evidence *despite attempts to obtain such negative evidence.* Thus, for a statement to be credible, not only must there by an absence of negative evidence, there must also have been attempts to falsify the statement. The credibility of a statement—its claim to be regarded as true—may therefore be said to depend on there having been, firstly, an adequate *number* of tests which could have falsified it. The credibility of the potato plant hypothesis depends on the number of attempts to grow potato plants in ashy soil without obtaining goodness of growth greater than that which was obtained in non-ashy soil.

Credibility also depends on there having been an adequate *variety* of tests which could have falsified it.

It would not be sufficient for the potato plant scientist simply to repeat, and go on repeating, his original experiment as earlier described, and thereby merely increase the number of cases where his measurements showed that the potato plants growing in ashy soil grew better than their counterparts in non-ashy soil. He must attempt to vary the conditions under which all the plants, both those in the ashy soil and in the control group, are grown to discover whether there are other alternative or additional factors which might have influenced the growth of the original single plant which he observed; other factors, that is, which might cause him to change or amen his hypothesis. (Such a factor might be the moisture content of the soil.) In his introduction to Popper's work, Magee gives an account of how doing this causes the amendment and improvement of an original hypothesis (7a). (See also p 123 ff.)

In brief, the problem of induction is that we cannot prove that a statement is true. What Popper argues is that the scientist, whenever he tests the statement by carrying out experiments or observations, is attempting to *disprove* the statement. Insofar as he fails to do so, he increases its credibility. We cannot prove that the Sun always rises in the east, implying as this statement does, that it will rise in the east tomorrow; but it is a highly credible statement, because of all the previous occasions which we know of when it might have risen in some other direction and has not done so.

It must be noted that it is an essential feature of Popper's philosophy that we *cannot know* and cannot prove that anything is *absolutely* true. We have not tried to discuss this point in detail here, but it is very important. It is also believed by scientists that there are fundamental limitations to what we *can* know, which are inherent in the nature of things. The most important example is the Principle of Uncertainty, which states that in some cases where there are two phenomena A and B, we can observe phenomenon A *or* we can observe phenomenon B, but that it is inherent in the relation of the two phenomena that we cannot observe them both simultaneously. It is partly as if we see two trains travelling in opposite directions simultaneously passing each other. We can continue watch either one train or the other, but not both. If we watch one, we are uncertain about the other. (This analogy omits an important aspect of the Principle, namely that it may be the act of observation itself which affects the phenomena and prevents their simultaneous observation).

Before continuing to the next point, we may refer back to the idea of four levels of inference: speculation, hypothesis, theory and law. This idea is not altered greatly in this alternative philosophy of science, except that the criterion by which inferences are adjudged to belong to these different levels is changed from one of amount of positive evidence or proof, to one of credibility or absence of negative evidence. We might thus state that a theory, as opposed to a hypothesis, is an inference which has been shown to be consistent with other theories about related matters. We might also point out that if theory A is credible in part because of its consistency with theory B, then theory B is credible in part because of its consistency with theory A: theories are mutually supporting in the matter of credibility. In practice, of course, it is not just a question of relationships between two theories, but among and between whole networks of interdependent theories.

The importance of social knowledge to science

We have tried to point out that inferences increase in credibility as they are subjected to (and are not falsified by) an increasing number and variety of tests. Also we have made the point that it should be possible for any competent scientist (*ie* for any scientist who is suitably conversant with the matter to which an inference relates) to examine and evaluate both the reasoning which produces the inferences (or which is used in the prediction of its consequences) and the methodology of the tests which produce the data or evidence which give it credibility. As part of this evaluation it may be deemed necessary for the tests to be repeated.

If *any* other competent scientist is to carry out further tests of an inference produced by a scientist (either by repeating the original test or by carrying out an alternative), or if the inference and the tests are to be evaluated by another scientist, it is necessary that *all* competent scientists should be informed of the inference and the tests. For all these other scientists to be informed about them for this purpose, it is necessary that details of them be recorded and made publicly available: *ie* it is essential that they become public knowledge. In practice in the modern scientific community, many or most of the other competent scientists are likely to be informed by the original scientist through what are called informal

75

channels (*eg* by correspondence or by the distribution of some preliminary report). This speeds up communication: however, such preliminary reports are not usually regarded as part of the permanent record of science —they are semi-social as opposed to social knowledge—and their distribution does not relieve the scientist of the obligation to use formal channels, such as periodicals, so that his hypothesis and test results are placed 'on record', and so become part of social knowledge. Not the least of the reasons for this is that the distribution of preliminary reports is, or tends to be, a selective procedure, and, therefore, not *all* competent scientists receive copies (8)

Reversing this argument, we can say that the existence and use of social knowledge is essential to the conduct of science. This point is made by many writers on science, and on its philosophy and history.

Social knowledge, World Three and Public Knowledge

We described at some length the idea that social knowledge is the knowledge possessed by a society and available to its members through its records; we have also distinguished between social knowledge thus defined, public knowledge in the sense in which that term is used by philosophers, and Public Knowledge in the sense in which that term is used by Ziman. We have also attempted to show that science depends for its continuing existence and activity on records. We shall now examine further some of the ideas which underlie the contention that there exists a distinct 'social' knowledge, and consider some of its properties. The discussion is, as mentioned earlier, largely drawn from Popper's ideas (World Three) and Ziman's notion of Public Knowledge, although the ideas are also found elsewhere implicitly or explicitly, *eg* in Merton and Piaget (9).

World Three

Popper (10) suggests that there are three 'Worlds':

World One—the world of things, of material objects: *eg* potato plants.

World Two—the world of minds in which ideas originate: *eg* the mind of the potato plant scientist who produced the hypothesis which is used as our example.

World Three—the world of the products of the mind: *eg* the potato plant hypothesis is the product of the potato plant scientist's mind; it originated there, and so is part of World Three.

Any example of what have elsewhere been described as artefacts and mentefacts belongs to World Three (referred to as the 'Third World' in earlier discussions by Popper). The ideas of tin kettles, of the pyramids built in ancient Egypt and elsewhere by ancient civilisations, of the Lunar Excursion Modules used to explore the Moon's surface, and of economic, social and political theories all must have originated in the minds of people: they are the products of minds and so belong to World Three. Popper also includes in World Three the product of non-human minds, so that the nests of birds (his own example), beavers' dams and beehives all belong to World Three. It also includes all social knowledge, because all knowledge which is recorded and made publicly available has, as we mentioned in chapter 3, obviously originated in the mind of some person. In our discussion of World Three we shall concentrate on that part of it which corresponds to social knowledge.

It is obvious that ideas—World Three—not only originate in minds but also continue to exist in minds: we are capable not only of thinking (originating ideas), but remembering (prolonging the existence of ideas). Much more important however is the notion that World Three can continue to exist independently of any human mind *if it is recorded.* For example, ancient Greek philosophy—the ideas of the ancient Greek philosophers—continues to exist, even though there was a long time during the Middle Ages, perhaps as much as a thousand years, during which much of it was unknown to any human mind and existed only in records. Other examples are the Rosetta Stone, which was known to exist for many years and was believed to contain ideas (knowledge), even though the markings on it were indecipherable; and the diary of Beatrix Potter, which was known to be the product of the authoress' mind, but because it was written in a code of her own devising, that particular part of World Three remained in existence independently of any human mind for decades until quite recently, when it was decoded. World Three, then, will survive:

if it is recorded;

if the records survive.

In discussing the idea of World Three in Popper's philosophy, Magee contrasts the knowledge which exists in the minds of people with the knowledge which exists in libraries. He states that the latter is more important because it survives better.

On the basis of these arguments, we may conclude that social knowledge has much greater durability than personal knowledge. The knowledge which exists only in the minds of people ceases to exist when the owners of the minds die. Social knowledge, however, can continue to exist even when all those who have ever known it have been dead for centuries.

There are two further points to be made in relation to World Three. We may note that it is not only ancient Greek philosophy which is part of World Three, but also ancient Greek drama and poetry. World Three consists not only of works produced in the mind by reason, but also works produced by imagination. We return to this point later. Secondly, there is a slight difference between World Three as it has been exemplified here, and social knowledge. Our definition of social knowledge stresses the availability of the knowledge; as our examples of Greek learning and Beatrix Potter's diary show, the idea of availability is not quite so necessary to Popper's conception of World Three (this point is mentioned by him however). The difference is comparatively trivial and unimportant to the general trend of our discussion.

World Two

World Two is the world of minds; two aspects of Popper's ideas in relation to it are relevant. Firstly, he suggests that the study of questions such as the meaning of 'I know' are concerned only with World Two, and are irrelevant to World Three: in the terms of this book, they are concerned only with personal, and not with social, knowledge (see chapter 4). Secondly, he suggests that the study of World Three may throw light on the nature of World Two: that understanding of social knowledge may help us to understand personal knowledge; but as part of the same thesis he suggests that the reverse is not true. This is contrary to the *modus operandi* of this book which in part is based on the belief that knowing about personal knowledge *can* help to provide insight into social knowledge. The reason for this divergence *may* be that Popper is concerned primarily with philosophy, whereas our scope includes experimental psychology, whose results are, at least in some respects, comparable to Popper's ideas about World Three.

Ziman's Public Knowledge

Ziman is largely concerned with scientific knowledge and he distinguishe very clearly between science and non-science (11). Nevertheless many of his ideas are valid for non-science as well as for science (as he himself suggests they might be); *eg* Watson and his colleagues arrive at similar conclusions for the social sciences (12).

In addition to the importance of the existence of Public Knowledge, Ziman emphasises the importance of its organisation. It may be said that there are three aspects to the organisation of Public Knowledge (the first of these is not, however, discussed by Ziman). They are:

organisation by creation;

self-organisation;

bibliographic organisation, including organisation in libraries.

Organisation by creation refers simply to the fact that the composition
of a document is a process of organisation and that documents, to be of
any use, must be organised. To put this at a ridiculous level, if I were
to sit and type out a suitable number of letter 'A's, then a suitable number of letter B's, and so on until I reached Z and the punctuation marks
(and left a few blank pages at the end to represent the spaces!) the resulting volume would not have contained any information for the reader.
It is the organisation of the letters into words, of the words into sentences,
the sentences into paragraphs and the paragraphs into chapters which give
documents their meaning.

Self-organisation refers to the fact that scientific documents and documents in other branches of learning contain, like this one, references to
other books and documents which their authors have used in the course
of their preparation. A whole chain of such references eventually results.
This is an important feature of scientific and other scholarship: the user,
having discovered one document which he thinks is relevant or pertinent
to his needs, is by this means enabled to find others. The references in a
document can, of course, refer only to its precursors: there are now, however, citation indexes (14) through which scientists and certain others
can, given knowledge of a particular document, find which are its successors, that is they can find the documents in which the particular document
is referred to (as opposed to those to which it itself refers). This, however,
is a special feature of bibliographical organisation. These references also
have the purpose of certifying that a statement made by the referring
author is correct: if he writes, 'Joe Bloggs claims . . .' he is expected to
give a reference to the document in which Joe Bloggs made this claim.

Bibliographic organisation is a term which we use to describe the fact
that when a document is made available (published), it will be included
in various lists, of which bibliographies proper, abstracting journals,
indexing journals, and information services which use computers for the
retrieval of documents, are important examples. These lists enable their
users to find documents on particular subjects, by particular authors, or
categorised in various other ways or combinations of ways. The arrangement and listing of documents which is performed by librarians is also a
very important part of the process.

Ziman claims that the importance of this organisation is such that
without it, scientific knowledge would not exist and science as an activity

would not be possible. To exist usefully knowledge must be recorded *and organised*. The idea might be expressed by saying that if the processes of self-organisation and bibliographical organisation did not exist, information would exist; but, because this information would not be available to its potential users, it would not constitute knowledge. Knowledge cannot exist without organisation. The same conclusion was reached in the examination of the psychological approach to personal knowledge. Further, we can link these ideas by referring to remarks which have been made about the process of drawing inferences being the same as (or an example of) the process of forming concepts; and to what we described as the first aspect of the organisation of Ziman's Public Knowledge—that composing or creating documents is itself a process of organisation.

The content of social knowledge

In the foregoing, we have made much use of the word 'ideas'. It would be wrong to think that social knowledge consists only of ideas, especially as elsewhere in this chapter we have mentioned a number of things which are properly parts of social knowledge, but which are not ideas. The following description is based on Popper's discussion of the contents of World Three and links parts of his discussion to terminology we have used earlier. Popper suggests (15) that World Three consists of:

problems
ideas
evidence
criticism

Using our potato plant example again, we may say that a 'problem' exists when the potato plant scientist asks himself why the original plant appeared to grow so much better than other plants (16). If he were to investigate the question by the experiment we described, he would include a statement of the problem in the document in which he reported the results of his experiment. This document would also contain the 'idea' that the growth was due to the nature of the soil in which the plant was growing. The word 'idea' refers to what we have discussed earlier, using then the term 'inferences'. The 'evidence' is the data resulting from experiments, or it might be reasoning which relates the hypothesis to other, more 'credible' statements. The idea and the evidence, as well as the problem, would be contained in the document produced by our potato plant scientist. As an example of 'criticism', another potato plant scientist might, perhaps, repeat the original experiment and find that, in the case of his plants, the presence of ash did not affect their growth. His document would therefore be a refutation or criticism of the idea in the document of the original scientist (but it would not be regarded as a criticism of the original scientist as a person or of his professional capabilities). The data contained in the second document might be referred to as counter-evidence.

The evaluation of the original scientist's idea or hypothesis will not be limited to a repetition of his first test: other scientists and perhaps the original scientist himself will try to conduct other tests of the idea (cf p 75), and there may also be criticism of the reasoning which is used in the explanation of the idea, or in relating the evidence to it. If the problem and the idea were regarded as of importance, there would eventually be a considerable number of documents describing the problem, the original idea, and new ideas, and containing evidence and criticism. These would all be interdependent: we can draw attention again to Ziman's point that they would be self-organised and bibliographically organised, and also to his emphasis on the importance of such organisation. In other words, social knowledge does not consist only of problems, ideas, evidence and criticism in isolation: it exists because the various parts are interdependent and organised.

Consensus

This, and our earlier reference to 'networks of interdependent theories', leads on to Ziman's idea of consensus. In the foregoing discussion we referred to documents produced by the original potato plant scientist, and subsequently by other potato plant scientists. These contained problems, ideas, evidence and criticism. They were the original reports of these things and typically, in science, they would appear as articles in periodicals. As well as articles in periodicals, however, Public Knowledge or social knowledge is contained in many other kinds of document. There are periodicals devoted to review articles, there are encyclopaedias; there are books which a specialist writes for other specialists (monographs) and books which a specialist or teacher writes for his pupils or students (textbooks).

It is with these that the idea of consensus originates. Although they may occasionally contain original problems, ideas and evidence, the function of such documents is not primarily to present original ideas for the first time, but to examine in relation to some topic or group of topics, all the problems, ideas, evidence and criticism; and especially to evaluate the various ideas in the light of the evidence and criticism. As Popper might express it, their function is to provide an insight into their credibility by revealing what is the consensus of competent opinion about them. There may be, for example, a problem to which no satisfactory idea relates and for which there is no known solution. There may be several ideas about the same problem which are, as it were, in competition: there may be different sets of evidence which seem to be contradictory. The purpose of the second kind of documents is to balance the different problems, ideas and evidence against each other, and by so doing reveal the consensus of expert opinion at that particular time. The consensus may be regarded as the state of knowledge at the time.

Obviously, the consensus changes: this point and its implications are discussed later. We should emphasise here that mere publication (or 'recording' in our definition of social knowledge) does not make some idea or problem part of the consensus: it has to be accepted as such. A review or textbook is normally expected to describe the consensus, but the extent to which it does is also a matter of judgement—or consensus. It should also be noted that Ziman suggests there are some areas of scholarship in which the idea of consensus is invalid, unrepresentative or inadequate (17); a point to be discussed.

Summary and conclusions

In this chapter, the nature of science and scientific method have been examined with the purpose of showing that the intended product of science is knowledge, and then of discussing the nature of that knowledge. Scientific knowledge may be considered as a set of interconnected, and mutually dependent and supportive, statements. These statements contain problems, ideas, evidence and criticism. Essentially they all refer to matters which can be tested. Tests can best be regarded as attempts to falsify an idea. According to the number and variety of tests to which it has been subjected, an idea may be referred to as a speculation, a hypothesis, a theory or a law. The results of tests are quantitatively determined. Test results, or data, and the arguments used to connect them with ideas, constitute evidence. Problems arise (for example) when an idea is falsified as the result of tests, or when there are several ideas, whose relations to the evidence are not at the time clear. Criticism may be concerned with ideas, with evidence, or with pointing out problems. It produces and reveals the consensus; that is, the balance of expert assessment in relation to the statements constituting any particular subset of scientific knowledge at a particular time. (The property of change is discussed later).

Other characteristics of the statements are that they are objective (independent of who made them), that there is a general preference for the idea which has the most simple relations to the evidence, and their probabilistic nature. In order that the statements may be generally available for criticism, and that ideas may be (further) tested, they must be available to all those in positions to criticise and test. For this reason, they are made public in documents; these documents are, in various ways, organised. Social knowledge generally (and not only scientific knowledge) is important because it has an existence independent of minds, and is thus more durable.

We referred to the idea in Popper's philosophy that nothing can be proved, and to the notion that there are fundamental limitations to knowledge. It is important for the non-scientist to realise that science is not seen as a means whereby everything there is to know will eventually be known. Indeed, experience as well as principle, seems to indicate that there are always 'problems'—knowledge is never complete.

NOTES AND REFERENCES

1 Readable introductory accounts include Bassey (1968), Bradbury (1969), Jevons (1973), Losee (1972) and Weatherall (1968). Hempel (1966) is an introduction suited to the needs of those who are embarking on a detailed study of the philosophy of science, and books such as Harré (1970), Hesse (1973), and Himsworth (1970) are more advanced. For the difference between science and technology see Price (1975) ch 6, p 125.

2 This account is based partly on Lee (1968); see also Magee (1973) p 56.

3 For detailed discussions of scientific inference see Hintikka (1970), Lakatos (1970) and Watanabe (1969).

4 Ziman (1968) p 125.

5 See however Mitroff (1974).

6 Mason (1966) p 110-115.

6a Watson (1971), Olby (1974). See also Mitroff (1974).

7 Korner (1973) p 87-90; Magee (1973) ch 2; Popper (1972) ch 1.

7a Magee (1973).

8 Meadows (1974) is a good readable introduction to scientific communication. Hanson (1971) is briefer. Nelson (1970) and Reuck (1967) are important collections of articles. Communication is also the topic of Ziman (1968) ch 6; Merta (1972) deals with informal communication, as does Gray (1975) ch 2.

9 Popper (1972); Ziman (1968); Piaget (1972); Merton (1973) p 23 and elsewhere. See also Brookes (1974).

10 Popper (1972) ch 3 and 4; Magee (1973) ch 4.

11 Ziman (1968) ch 2.

12 Watson (1973).

13 Ziman (1968) ch 6.

14 *Science Citation Index, Social Science Citation Index.* Such indexes have been a feature of legal 'social knowledge' for many years.

15 Popper (1972) p 111.

16 Compare ch 5, note 26b.

17 Ziman (1968) p 8 ff.

Chapter 7

THE SOCIAL ENVIRONMENT OF KNOWLEDGE
AND ITS INFLUENCE

INTRODUCTION: In this chapter, we examine the influence of social factors on knowledge, by considering ideas drawn from social psychology (the study of the psychology of groups of people, as opposed to the psychology of individual persons), as well as ideas from the sociology of knowledge itself (1). Our interest is still with social knowledge, but in order to consider some important aspects of the topic we concern ourselves first with knowledge which in various ways might be regarded as personal rather than social, and with situations in which the idea of the availability of knowledge through records is not always relevant. Later, some of these ideas are related to social, recorded knowledge; and lastly there are examples of the way in which society may attempt to determine the knowledge which is available to its members.

Part of our definition of social knowledge is that it is knowledge possessed by a society or social system. Numerous different kinds of social systems exist. Nations are social systems, as are smaller political units. Practitioners of trades, crafts and professions also form social systems of greater or lesser degrees of formality, and with more or less clearcut boundaries. It is also possible to regard social classes as subsystems of the communities to which they belong. It is relevant to point out that geographical, climatic and other environmental factors are important in determining the nature of the social systems themselves. The various categories which are given here by no means form a comprehensive list, and there are, in fact, numerous inter-related ways in which it is possible to classify social systems. The intention is only to point out that there are different social systems, that social systems may be categorised in different ways, and that they exist in different environments.

Social systems and personal knowledge
It is obvious that the social system to which an individual belongs will influence his personal knowledge, and indeed the point has already been

considered (p 53), where the influence of the South African social system, with its rigid racial classification, was mentioned in relation to the ability of individual South Africans to perceive shades of grey between black and white. Their ability, or lack of it, reflects the knowledge which they possess; because the ability of an individual to perceive, depends on the knowledge which he already possesses.

It is, however, an oversimplification to regard the individual as belonging to one and only one social system: in fact he belongs to a number of social systems (this is the idea of partial inclusion in systems theory), and his membership of each and every one of them will influence his personal knowledge. The reader can verify this in relation to the writer, who is a member of the following social systems, among others: the profession of librarianship, the community of polytechnic lecturers, the system formed by the inhabitants of the north-east of England, and to a lesser extent, the international astronomical community. All of these systems have influenced his personal knowledge, as can be seen in his choice of examples.

It is necessary here to make the general point that knowledge consists not only or even most importantly of knowledge of 'facts' (such as 'Mr Smith lives at 24 Bloggs Street'), but also of beliefs ('I think Mr Smith is a greengrocer'), opinions ('Mr Smith is likeable') and prejudices ('Mr Smith must be mean, because he's a Scotsman, and all Scotsmen are mean'). These of course are not distinct categories; they merge into each other and what in one society may be accepted as fact ('All Jews are usurers') will in another society be regarded as prejudice. In essence, as we try to demonstrate elsewhere, facts are facts only because they are accepted as such.

Knowledge, language and social systems

One of the principal influences of a social system on knowledge is the language used within the social system (2). By this we do not refer merely to the fact that within the French social system the French language is used, but to the fact that because the French social system is different from the Swedish one (and because the environments of these systems, France and Sweden, are different also) the vocabulary which is available in French is different from the vocabulary which is available in Swedish. The syntax (or grammar) used in different languages is also sometimes important.

The social systems in France and Sweden are, however, too alike, and too similar to the British social system for it to be easy to illustrate the various pieces of evidence which language gives us in relation to the influence of social systems on knowledge. Here, however, are two examples. Firstly, the trades of bricklayer and plasterer are not separate in Sweden as they are in France and Britain, and so the Swedish language has only one word (which means wallworker) to cover both activities. Secondly there is a story, perhaps apocryphal, which illustrates both this point and the fact that individuals belong to more than one social system, all of which affect their personal knowledge. When General de Gaulle visited the Paris Observatory, he rather critically asked why so many of the publications produced by the astronomers were written in English. The reply was that if they were not, they were unlikely to be read by non-French astronomers. French astronomers belong to both the French social system and the international community of astronomers which is also, of course, a social system. In the choice of language for their publications, they are influenced much more by the custom of the latter than the demands of the former, even though the French government actively and officially encourages the use of the French language.

Environment

One way in which language reflects the relationship between the knowledge of a society and the society itself, is the extent to which the language reflects the environment in which the society exists. Thus, in a language used by the Eskimos, there are numerous different terms used for snow. The language used by desert Arabs has a vocabulary of about 600 different terms for camels and things associated with them. By contrast there is no Eskimo word for camel, and the desert Arabs have no word for snow (3).

The existence of a word in a language is evidence that the users of the language have some concept in common about which they need to communicate. That is, the concept is an item of shared knowledge. The existence of several different words for different things means that users the the must be able to perceive, as distinct and different from each other, the things for which they use the words. We would perceive one camel as pretty much the same as every other camel. Perhaps, given the opportunity, we might be able to distinguish the sexes, but this is likely to remain the limit of our ability. Desert Arabs, however, have numerous different words relating to camel pregnancy because they can perceive numerous different things about camel pregnancy, most of which we would not recognise. This and numerous other things reveal how knowledgeable the desert Arabs are about camels, which is simply a reflection of their environment, as also our ignorance of the same subject is a reflection of our (camel-less) environment.

Language and perception

There are, however, examples of the influence of language on perception which seem to be independent of the physical environment of the social system in which the language is used. The ability to perceive colours provides an instance. The language of the Navaho Indians of North America is one of several which have a vocabulary of colours quite different from that of English. In such languages there may be no word that corresponds to our 'green', and hues which we would identify as 'green' are identified by their speakers with a word which also represents hues which would be called 'brown' by English speakers. Unless the speakers of these languages have vocabulary which enables them to distinguish between hues in this way, it is unlikely that they will learn to perceive the difference between them. In the case of the Navaho Indians, a considerable number of them also speak English, and tests were carried out which showed that those who spoke English in addition to Navaho perceived colours differently from those who spoke only Navaho. This, it is assumed, is the result of the influence of their awareness of the different colour values which are used in the English language, rather than any other possible factor (4).

Language: reason and time

Language also affects the ability to reason. If we were desert Arabs, we would, as children, have learnt the fifty different words associated with camel pregnancy, and thus formed the concepts which our parents associated with those words. Just as the children of British parents learn the words 'car', 'van', 'bus', and 'lorry', American children will have learnt different words and slightly different concepts. Having acquired the concepts related to camels, we would then be able to ascribe the behaviour of a particular camel to the fact that it was in such-and-such state of pregnancy. Because we do not have these concepts, we cannot reason along these lines, at least not with any degree of exactitude (5). Later we shall re-examine this point in relation to social knowledge of a kind which is rather more familiar to us.

Another example of the influence of a social system through the language it uses, on the knowledge possessed by its members, relates to the idea of the passage of time. This involves not only the vocabulary but also to the syntax of the language. As speakers of an Indo-European language we are used to the idea of what may be called a 'three-tense' situation: we have a past, a present and a future. As a result, to our way of thinking, 'time flies like an arrow'. In very many other languages the situation is quite different. They have what might be called a 'two-tense' situation, and think only of 'now' and 'then'— that is, for the users of those languages, it is either the present, now, or it is some other time, then. They do not distinguish between the past and the future, and time does not fly like an arrow but is cyclical or circular.

If it is summertime, we consider the previous spring is in the past and that the next spring is in the future; and we regard the spring just past and the spring of next year as being two different times, in which different events may take place. To those who use the two-tense languages, the summertime is 'now' and the spring which has passed and the spring which is to come are (or is) the same time—in which the same things happen. The reader may have some difficulty in comprehending this; that is, in itself, a sufficient example of the way in which we think—our knowledge—is influenced by the way in which we can express ourselves— our language. By way of emphasis, there is at least one language—that used by the Trobriand Islanders—which has no tenses at all; and the thinking of those people seems not to involve the concept of time (6).

The reader may ask whether this is at all relevant to the kind of know-ledge which appears in libraries. The writer has at times asked himself the same question and, having been an astronomical librarian, was quite surprised to discover that this particular point, the conception of time, is directly relevant to astronomical literature. One major topic in astro-nomy is cosmology—the problem of the origin and development of the universe as a whole. For this question even to occur to anyone, it is necessary that they have the idea of the passage of time in the western, Indo-European, sense. If one has the 'now and then' concept of time, the question of the 'origin' of anything, including the Universe, assumes much less significance. Referring to a popular conundrum, in the 'now and then' sense of time, there is simply an infinitely recurring cycle of chickens and eggs, and the problem of which came first simply does not arise. The problem only arises when there is a distinction between the past and the future. There are many oriental astronomers who have made considerable contributions to the science—but few of them have appeared interested in cosmological problems. This has been explained simply on the basis that the cultures of these scientists are among those which have (as can be seen from their languages) the 'now and then' sense of time (7).

Non-linguistic examples

It is not only through the medium of language that a social system exerts an influence on the knowledge that its members possess; it is quite possible to demonstrate the influence of a system on the knowledge of its members without reference to language.

Referring again to our example of black and white in South Africa, it has been demonstrated that in South Africa (and also in the southern states of the USA) one of the first things that a person recognises (or perceives) in relation to another person is the colour of his skin. In the different social system of northern Africa, where for centuries there has been inter-marriage between the races, it seems that the colour of skin is hardly perceived at all—it has little or no social significance (8).

Professions and trades were mentioned in the introduction as being examples of social systems, and they too exert an influence on the knowledge and perception of their members. Various comments made by members of different professions on the writer's home illustrate this. At different times, people have commented that it is a good building. When asked what he meant, the architect said that it was well laid-out, well planned. Asked the same question, a builder said that he noticed that the bricks which had been used were of a very expensive variety. A neighbour who works in the building supply trade meant by the same remark that the fitments, like door-handles and light switches, were of good quality. Lest it be thought that the writer lives in some kind of palace, the buildings inspector for the local council has remarked that the house is bad, in that it is too close to its neighbour. All of these people have been influenced in what they perceived about the same thing by the occupation in which they are active.

The social systems to which we belong affect not only what we perceive, but also what we remember. The Swazis of South Africa are a tribe renowned for their feats of memory, and provide two instances of how memory is affected by society. The tribe exists by herding animals and their prodigious feats of memory are related entirely to this activity, on which their livelihood depends. In other respects, their ability to remember is not extraordinary. The other example relates to a visit to London made some years ago by some tribal chiefs, for whom the outstanding memory was of policemen stopping the traffic at road junctions. The reason for this seeming so important was because the position adopted by the policemen for this purpose is the same as the Swazi gesture of greeting.

Non-recorded social knowledge

Our definition of social knowledge includes the idea that such knowledge is available through records. In the light of the examples given so far, it is perhaps necessary to recall that, while this aspect of it is largely true for literate societies and is a very important and necessary distinction in an examination of the nature of knowledge as it is found in libraries, nevertheless it is not, and cannot, be valid for societies which are non-literate and which therefore have no (or only a few) records (9). In such societies the memories of the members replace, or correspond to, the records possessed by a literate society. (Historically the statement should be reversed because the development of the creation and use of records and literacy occur subsequent to the use of memory.)

We gave the memories of the Swazi tribesmen earlier as an example, and drew attention to the fact that the things which they could remember were the things which are vital to their continued existence as herdsmen. They retain this capability because of the non-existence of means of making records. The contents of this book bear to the writer the same relationship as the memories which a Swazi tribesman has of the positions of waterholes bear to the tribesman: the writer depends for his living on them. Unlike the Swazi, however, he does not, because he does not have to, remember all the details; those are to be found in his notes.

What is true of the individual is also true of the society. For example, until very recently, technological societies depended to no small extent on the use of tables of figures, such as logarithmic tables (this dependence has decreased with the availability of computers and other calculators). Although there are people who have memorised these tables, they did not need to do so because it is so easy, convenient and cheap to use the printed tables. If means of recording the values in the tables did not exist, however, it would have been necessary (and much more general) to do so.

Social systems and recorded knowledge

Social knowledge can exist without the existence of records, and without the existence of libraries. But the existence of records has certain advantages. It avoids reliance on memory and it probably means that a society can preserve much more knowledge than would otherwise be possible. Even if the records are not permanent and indestructible, they are at least durable, as was discussed when the notion of Popper's World Three was examined. It is almost certainly the case that unless records existed it would be impossible for modern technological societies to exist. In relation to this last point, these societies also depend on the fact that the mass of the population has the potential to use the records; that is, they depend (or until very recently have depended) on mass-literacy.

The facts that records replace memory, and that libraries are places where the records are preserved, give rise to the idea (which the reader will find in several of the books to which he is referred) that libraries are the corporate memories of society.

Social knowledge (and 'knowledge' here retains the broad sense of including beliefs, opinions and prejudices as well as 'facts') is like personal knowledge in that it is influenced by the social system which possesses it. It is obvious that this must be so, because, firstly, of the influence of the social system on the personal knowledge of individuals within it, and, secondly, because the personal knowledge (one might say personal knowledges) of individuals are the source of social knowledge, which is created each time some individual records part of his personal knowledge.

The cosmology example is a partial example of this. We now give some further examples of how social systems have influenced the social, recorded knowledge within their possession.

Reasoning and social knowledge

The first example is based on an idea already put forward: that the ability to reason is influenced by the language of those who do the reasoning, which is itself a reflection of the social system to which they belong. The readers of this book probably studied mathematics ('the science of reasoning', as it is sometimes referred to) while at school, and they would have been concerned with three branches: geometry, algebra and arithmetic. It may have been pointed out to them, or they may have realised, that geometry was devised by the ancient Greeks (or at least by adherents of Greek civilization) such as Euclid, Pythagoras and Apollonius. It may not have been pointed out to them, however, that the development of algebra and the methods they learned to use in arithmetic were not devised until about six or seven centuries ago; that is, about two thousand years after the Greeks had busied themselves with geometry and had made social knowledge of their geometrical propositions. This startling time-lag is due to the influence of language.

92

The reader is asked to write down the answer to the following calculation:

$5 \times 6 =$

The answer is (we hope) thirty, which presumably has been written as 30. What would you have done, however, if you had not known about the zero, or the fact that the position of the digits is important, *ie* that '03' is not the same quantity as '30'?

The point of this demonstration is that our modern methods of arithmetic are dependent on the use of a system of numerals (and numerals systems are a form of language) which features the use of a symbol for zero and in which the position of the digits is relevant. The Greeks did not possess such a system—they used a system which resembles the Roman system (I, II, III, IV, V, VI, . . . X, L, C, D, M, etc) and were, therefore, not able to perform arithmetical calculations in the way with which we are now familiar. Their system of numbers also lacked a symbol for an unknown quantity (for which we generally use the letter 'x') which is essential if calculations (reasoning) are to be carried out by algebraic methods.

It was only when the Arabs adopted or invented the use of a system of numerals (which we adopted from them and call arabic numerals) that it becomes possible to perform intricate arithmetical calculations; and it was only because of the adoption of a symbol for the unknown quantity that algebra (which is a word of Arabic derivation) could be developed. This is in contrast to geometry which can be (and was) developed without the use of such numerals. Thus part of the social knowledge of the Greeks was geometry, because it could be discussed in terms of the language available to them: but arithmetic and algebra as we know them were alien to the Greeks, not because they lacked the mental ability, but because they lacked the symbols—the language—which are necessary for these forms of calculation (10).

Commonsense

The foregoing discussion enables us to make a slight divergence to consider a point which is sometimes raised by students in connection with the matters discussed in this book. Is not all of this, they ask, just comm sense or common knowledge? To some extent the answer is simply 'yes'; but the other part of the answer is to ask what is meant by common sense or common knowledge, and then to point out that notions of commonsense and common knowledge are not as simple or commonsense as might have been thought.

93

Firstly, the things which are common knowledge have all been invented or discovered by somebody at some time. Prior to that time nobody knew them and, even subsequently, it was probably some time before they became sufficiently widely available for them to be regarded as common. In writing down the answer to the multiplication of the number five by the number six, it is common knowledge that one writes down the figure zero, and then the symbol for three to the left of the zero. This was not, however, common knowledge to the Greeks or the Romans; nor indeed to the medieval merchants and bankers, who had to invent special calculating devices in order to perform the necessary arithmetic, even though, in their case, the method had been invented and was used in lands where some of them traded.

Further it is part of the purpose of this book and of this chapter to show that common knowledge is not quite so 'common' as might be imagined. In the UK, it is common knowledge that if you have a serious accident you will be taken to hospital to receive the necessary treatment regardless of your apparent financial position or whether you are medically insured against such an event. Such 'knowledge' is not however 'common' throughout the USA, where your ability to pay may be assessed before the necessary treatment is decided on. What is common knowledge to an Arab is quite uncommon to an Eskimo. Lastly, it is only by questioning what constitutes 'common knowledge' that we will be able to discover whether it is 'true' or not, and to improve our knowledge (11).

History as social knowledge

As a subject, history provides numerous examples of the effect that society can have on the recorded views and interpretations of events and personalities. The same events and personalities are likely to be interpreted in different ways by different writers, because they belong to different social systems. In part, at least, this may be done unconsciously; because the writers are themselves unaware of the influences which have acted on them. It may also result from the fact that their membership of a particular system determines the sources which are available to them; and in part it may be because the writers are aware that they are writing for readers who belong to a particular social system. Whatever the reasons, the result is that if an event is part of the history of two different social systems, the place that the event has in the social knowledge of the systems may be quite different.

English and French history, especially as presented in the school textbooks of the two nations, provide a very clear instance. The reader is

94

probably familiar with the names Poitiers, Crécy and Agincourt, and associates them with notable English victories in the Hundred Years War. If this is so, it is because they appear in English history textbooks in this light. If the corresponding French books are examined, it will be found that these battles are not mentioned; or if they are, they are described as minor skirmishes, unimportant in the overall trend of events.

Similarly there are a number of famous English admirals who are often regarded in the less scholarly versions of English history as important figures in the development of English sea power. More detailed examination often reveals (in cases such as that of Hawkins) that these admirals were little better than pirates and that there was very little moral justification for their activities, which would have been condemned if the admirals had not happened to be English. Their relation to the society of their day seems often to have been similar to the relation of aircraft hijackers to present-day society; their activities are meritorious only if you are a fervent believer in the causes which they claim to support.

It is not only between nations as social systems that differences may arise in the recorded interpretations of history. It can happen between different subsystems within the same nation. For many years the history of the southern states of the USA was written by whites. Recently, however, it has been taken up by black historians, who have discovered that the white authors have ignored certain crucial aspects of the topic and have presented a biased interpretation of others. Similarly, the interpretations of the events which comprised the settling of whites in the American West, depends very largely on whether the interpreter is white, or an American Indian; and the history of these events is also being revised (12).

It is not only the past which is subject to different interpretations; it happens also with current events. The best example of this in the writer's experience occurred when in his newspaper he read two discussions in successive weeks of the same set of statistics, one written by a Conservative and the other by a Labour Member of Parliament. They were equally convincing articles, even though they were diametrically opposed in their assessments of what the figures implied and what action should be taken! Although there is a mass of scholarly and semi-popular literature on this subject, and on the influence of mass-communication media, such as television, on the knowledge possessed by members of a particular society and on the structure of the society, we do not propose to examine the topics in detail here.

The examples given of different interpretations and presentations of the same historical events, arise from causes which to some extent are natural and inevitable (and the same may be said for some modern examples). It is scarcely to be expected that English historians concerned with the Elizabethan era will not be predisposed to ideas which suggest that it was a golden age. Again, it may require more effort on an English historian's part to regard the Hundred Years War as a lost cause for England, than is required by a French historian to present the same war as a victory for his countrymen (none of this is to deny that historians attempt to be objective in their assessments).

In the previous discussion, great use has been made of the word 'influence', and this does seem to be a very reasonable description of the process generally involved. There are, however, instances in which the word 'influence' is misleading, because, in fact, the situation is one of 'control'; that is, where one section of a society attempts to regulate the knowledge available to and possessed by the other members (13). Those who are in positions to exercise such control are those in authority, or those who have the ear of authority. The following two examples are given because they are cases in which the knowledge that was subject to control was scientific, and as we have discussed earlier, this kind of knowledge is supposed to be objective and not subject to influence or control; certainly not to the kind of control which can be exercised by political means.

Galileo

Galileo Galilei was a 16th century Italian who is renowned for his contributions to the sciences of astronomy and mechanics, to the development of scientific techniques, and also for his contribution to the 'traditional' scientific method described in the previous chapter. In order to understand how his work came to be affected by the politics of his day, it is necessary to know something of those politics. This 'nutshell' account is not, we hope, too distorted. In Italy in Galileo's time there were two powerful political forces: the Church, which was authoritarian, with part of its teaching at the time founded not only on Scripture, but also on the writings of such ancients as Ptolemy and Aristotle. Discussion of the ideas of these ancients was not forbidden, but it was limited to scholars, and was conducted in the then language of scholarship, Latin. The other force (more precisely a frequently changing alliance of several different forces) was the rich merchant class in cities like Florence,

Venice and Padua. The merchants were knowledgeable, cultured, and open to new ideas and they had a relationship with the Church of differing degrees of harmony at different times. They lacked however one attribute of the Church's scholars: they could not read, write or converse easily in Latin.

Galileo became enmeshed in the political situation, not because of the novelty of his ideas, nor because they challenged the statements of the ancients as these were accepted (and disseminated) by the Church, but because, by writing in the vernacular Italian, he made his ideas available to the population at large and to the merchant class in particular. Thus, it was felt, he put the authority of the Church at risk. He was at best tactless and at worst malicious in other features of the presentation of his ideas and, as a result, the Church did its utmost to prevent their propagation to the extent of forcing a public retraction from him. This is probably the first attempt to control the spread of scientific knowledge (14).

Lysenko and Soviet agriculture, 1925-1965

It is possible to distinguish two approaches to the improvement of agricultural methods and the development of new varieties of plants with qualities which will result in increased crops. On the one hand, there is what may be called the scientific approach; this takes the results of scientific experimentation and attempts to apply them to the needs of practical agriculture. It is largely based on the science of genetics as founded by a man called Gregor Mendel. On the other hand, there is what might be called the craft tradition, which attempts to examine, improve and refine traditional methods. The two approaches need not be regarded as opposed to each other; they both have advantages and disadvantages, the details of which need not concern us here. What is important in the present context is that the results obtained by either approach must be subjected to the same process of objective evaluation as that which was discussed in our description of scientific method.

One of the clearest instances of scientific knowledge becoming not merely influenced, but actually dominated, by political forces, is the development of Soviet agriculture between the years 1925 and 1965. During this period the full force of the Soviet political system, including the personal support of Stalin, was put behind the agricultural ideas of one particular man, Lysenko. These ideas belonged to what we have called the craft tradition, and were put forward in direct opposition to the theories of the Mendelian scientists. The hypothesis for which Lysenko is especially noted is the idea of vernalisation, whereby the

97

seeds of winter wheat are soaked and chilled, enabling them (it was claimed) to be planted in the spring and produce a crop. Another idea was a tree planting scheme which, it was hoped, would improve the climate for agriculture.

There are four notable features of Lysenko's ideas and the way in which he put them forward. Firstly, he claimed that his proposals would obtain quick results, as compared with the Mendelian approach. Secondly, his claims were not validated. When they were first brought to public attention, an investigatory commission was established, but favourable reports of its findings were issued before its tests were complete (and perhaps even before they were begun). Thirdly, he campaigned for support for his ideas, and used the press, in ways which were those of the politician rather than of the scientist or technologist. Fourthly, having gained support and having been placed in a position of considerable power, he used this power to stifle criticism of his ideas. In fact, political dogma was allowed to hold sway over the scientific ideal of objectivity, to the extent that one of the leading Soviet Mendelians died in a prison camp in 1944, and the institute in which genetics research was carried out in the Soviet Union was closed in 1948.

It was not until the early 1960s that official support was withdrawn from Lysenko. Although the reason for this was, in part, his inability to produce figures which supported his ideas, the fact that figures should be demanded of him and that his failure to produce these should be a matter of critical discussion, are only signs of the basic reason for Lysenko's fall from grace—namely, a changing political situation. Lysenko rose to a position of technological authority through politics rather than through technological brilliance, and he fell from that position for the same reason. Whilst he had authority he used it to control what was regarded as knowledge in the Soviet Union, even though this knowledge was in an area where knowledge is supposed to be objective and free from any other influence other than the results of objective reasoning and experimentation (15).

Conclusions

The instances which we have cited, and the reasoning which accompanies them, are only examples of the kind of discussion which is used when considering the relation between societies and knowledge. They are intended to be typical, and are not isolated cases. We could easily find other examples by delving into the literature of social anthropology, or by considering the history of some sciences (such as psychology) whose development has tended to occur within national or linguistic boundaries (thus German and American psychology were quite different for several decades). Also, differences in moral and ethical knowledge (or belief) have purposely not been examined, but it is assumed that the reader is at least aware that different societies have different creeds, and that what is 'known' to be ethical or justifiable in one society, or kind of society, may be 'known' to be unjustifiable (because immoral) in other societies.

Allowing for the fact that it is not possible (or perhaps necessary) to discuss every facet of the problem, nor to cite every instance, it is reasonable to derive the following conclusions from our examination:

1 Knowledge is influenced by the society in which it exists.

2 This is true both for the personal knowledge of the individual members of the society, and for the social knowledge possessed by the society collectively (and in the latter case, it is true both where the knowledge exists in the memories of members of the society and where it exists in records).

3 Various factors affect the relationship between the society and the knowledge which it possesses. No attempt has been made to identify these factors specifically, but consideration of the discussion suggests four such factors: the geographical environment of the society, its political structure, the language it uses, and perhaps also its history.

4 The fact that different societies possess different knowledge is often due to processes which occur naturally, inevitably and perhaps even subconsciously: that is they are not the result of different policies or conscious, explicitly stated decisions.

5 It is, however, possible that what is regarded as knowledge within a society may be deliberately controlled by political means and for political purposes—the term 'political' being used in quite a wide sense.

In general it seems reasonable to conclude that knowledge, or what is regarded as knowledge, is affected, if not determined, by the society in which it exists.

NOTES AND REFERENCES

1 Recommended texts in social psychology are Lindesmith (1968), Sampson (1971) and Lindgren (1973). Merton (1973) is a useful, but specialist, compendium in which part 1 deals with the sociology of knowledge in general.

2 Carroll (1964), Hilgard (1971) p 286, Lindesmith (1968) p 131ff, Potter (1960) ch 11 and 12, Rowan (1973) ch 4 and p 159ff. Whorf (1956) and Hoijer (1954) are standard references—the idea is often

referred to as the Whorf, or Whorf-Sapir, hypothesis. Lindgren (1973) p 318ff suggests that the importance of language should not be over-emphasised. Merton (1973) p 25-26 includes a description of the effect of the Chinese language.

3   Lindesmith (1968) p 28.

4   Lindesmith (1968) p 150.

5   Lindesmith (1968) p 131ff.

6   Lee (1950).

7   Metz (1972).

8   Lindesmith (1968) p 149ff; p 161ff. See also Deregowski (1972).

9   Riesman (1970) examines the differences between societies depending on the spoken word and societies depending on print.

10   Mason (1956) p 33, 66-67, 87. Bronowski (1974) and the BBC television programme on which it was based.

11   Lindgren (1973) p 6-8.

12   Lindesmith (1968) p 169ff; Merton (1973) p 134-135; Cooke (1973) and the series of BBC television programmes.

13   See also Merton (1973) p 257-260.

14   Mason (1956) p 120-129; Geymonat (1965).

15   Medvedev (1969); Huxley (1949); and a BBC television programme (Jan 1975).

Chapter 8

GROWTH OF KNOWLEDGE I
REASONS AND MEASUREMENTS

INTRODUCTION: In this chapter and the next, we shall examine one of
the principal, and perhaps most obvious features of knowledge—the fact
that it increases, or grows. In this chapter we are concerned with the
reasons for the growth of knowledge, with the means by which it can be
measured, and with the results of some measurements. In the next chapter
we comment on and discuss these measurements and their implications (1).

Why does knowledge grow?

Of the numerous reasons for the growth of knowledge, one is quite
simple: knowledge, and new knowledge, are essential for man's survival,
in either the individual or the collective sense. Indeed, information has
been described as the fifth need of man, ranking after air, water, food and
shelter. As an example, there are experiments which have shown that few
people can endure much more than twenty-four hours of being deprived
of all sensations (2).

Apart from such drastic cases however, it is obvious that everyone
needs a certain amount of knowledge to survive in the daily business of
living. The writer, in order to survive, needs to go to work; to go to work,
he has to travel by train; to travel by train, he has to know the times of
the trains which will get him to work on time. Moreover he has each year
to acquire new knowledge relating to the annual changes in the times of
the trains. If he drove to work, it would be necessary for his survival (in
a more immediate way) to know that he should drive on the left side of
the road.

Society is equally affected by this absolute necessity to know and to
acquire new knowledge. Modern industrial society needs to know about
sources of fuel as has recently been demonstrated so dramatically. It
needs to acquire new knowledge of both the alternative sources of the
fuels which it already uses, and of alternative fuels and their safe use, if it
is to survive in anything like its present form, or degree of comfort. A

101

three months examination of the more serious newspapers would provide a long list of similar examples of the need for knowledge and increased knowledge on the part of the society of which we are part (3).

Curiosity

Another reason for the growth of knowledge is that man is an enquiring animal; quite apart from the knowledge essential for survival, individual men are interested in themselves and the world which surrounds them. They have not been satisfied with knowing where the next meal is coming from; they have asked how it got there. This knowledge may be useful in ensuring future meals, but originally the question was asked out of mere curiosity: why and how does a plant grow? Astronomical investigations may have been necessary for the ancient Egyptians, so that they could devise a calendar for use in developing their agricultural method it was, however, curiosity (even more than national pride) that made man, six thousand years later, go to the Moon.

Numbers

Another fundamental reason for the growth of knowledge is also simple there are now more people alive to be curious, and to know things, than there were before (4). This is true of the present day; it is also true of practically any time in the history of the human race (possible exceptions being the times of the great plagues, such as the Black Death). There is no need to go into details of world population growth, but it is perhaps worth pointing to the scale of this growth. For example, when the United States of America was founded, the electoral register was numbered in thousands (700,000); now it is measured in millions. In Great Britain, the figures are not so dramatic, but even so, the writer has, in 1976, five times as many compatriots as he would have had if he had lived in 1801. During his lifetime, world population will double.

It is not simply mere numbers which have produced increased knowledge. There are other reasons, all of which depend ultimately on the fact that man is a social animal, and that individual men rarely live in isolation from their fellows (5).

Differentiation and specialisation

The first of these reasons may be called social differentiation (6). As we remark elsewhere, societies are social *systems*, and as systems develop, they inevitably become more complex, and the individual parts or members become more and more dissimilar in the functions they perform within the society. Thus, in a primitive society, we might imagine that the basic unit is the extended family of parents, children and grandparents. This unit will do everything necessary for its own survival: collect or produce food, make its own clothes, build its own shelters, make its own tools and so on. When the community becomes larger we find that specialists emerge: there are specialist hunters and farmers, garment makers, builders, and specialist makers of tools such as potters and metal-workers. These specialists are dependent on each other and on each other's knowledge. The farmer depends on the smith and his knowledge for the plough-shares which he uses, and the smith depends for his food on the farmer's knowledge of the use of the plough-share. At different stages there are different sizes of communities and different degrees of specialisation.

This trend continues to the present day. The profession of librarianship can claim to be 100 years old. The first full-time school of librarianship in Great Britain was founded in the early 1920s (7). By 1947, about twelve people were employed full-time in the teaching of professional skills; currently there are about three hundred. Up until about 1960, most teachers of librarianship were expected to teach any aspect of the subject as the occasion demanded. With the increased numbers they began to specialise, and currently very few of the three hundred would regard himself as being competent to teach all aspects of librarianship; he would not want to, nor, indeed, would it be necessary for him to be able to do so. The larger the number of people there are doing any job, the greater is the opportunity for the individual to become a specialist in some particular aspect of it.

The result of the process of social differentiation is, then, that there is increasing specialisation. The result of increased specialisation is that the individual is able to develop an increased knowledge in depth of his particular specialisation, be it the manufacture of plough-shares or the ability to teach the construction and maintenance of library catalogues. At the same time, the range or width of the individual's knowledge is increasingly restricted: the smith will not be able to learn all that the farmer knows (and will not need to know it), and the teacher of cataloguing may become quite out of date in his knowledge of library classification systems, in which he may at one time have regarded himself as an expert.

The social result of the increased depth of knowledge of individuals is that new subjects (or trades and professions) are evolved. The trade of smith develops from the existence of specialist smiths and from the need for them to pass on their specialist knowledge to their successors. Two different processes are involved in this development or evolution of new subjects.

Fission and fusion

The first of these is known as fission, which as the name implies, is the splitting of an existing subject into a number of (narrower) subjects, as, for example, the development of optics, acoustics, mechanics, hydro-dynamics, etc, by their splitting off from the parent science of physics. The parent subject of librarianship has produced, or been split into, narrower specialisations such as access to information, technical services, library management, and so on. The second process is called fusion, and again, as implied by the name, it involves the merging of ideas from two or more parent subjects to form a new specialised subject. Biological ideas were merged with ideas from physics to form the new subject biophysics, and their merger with concepts from chemistry similarly gave rise to the subject of biochemistry. In librarianship, the application of statistical techniques to measurements made of the use of documents has resulted in the study now referred to as bibliometrics; and the combination of knowledge of existing library techniques and of computer science and technology has produced the subject of 'library mechanisation', which now appears in various guises and with various names in library school syllabi and to which specialist journals are devoted (8).

Increased population, then, has of itself produced increased knowledge in one sense—that of there being, simply, more people around to know things. Moreover, the increased population has meant that the social systems into which the population has organised itself have also grown larger, and inevitably therefore more complex. This has produced in-creased specialisation in the members of those societies, which in turn has produced increases in the knowledge possessed by the societies.

Increased production

Another reason for the growth of knowledge is that as societies develop, their methods of production become more efficient (9). This, therefore, allows them to reduce that proportion of population directly engaged in the production of the goods necessary for the sustenance of the members of the society. There is evidence for this in the history of the ancient civilisations of Babylonia, Assyria, Egypt and Greece; in the development of European civilisation from the Middle Ages to the present day; in modern society, and also in 'developing countries' in Africa and Asia with their new educational systems and universities. Figure 1 shows an example of this: the application of new agricultural techniques has released an increasing proportion of the population of the USA from agricultural work. The dashed line on the figure represents the numbers

104

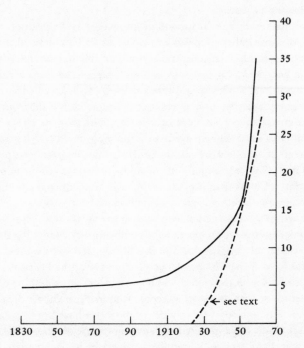

Figure 1: Numbers of persons supported by one farm worker
in the USA, 1830-1970.
Source: US Dept of Agriculture, 1966 (*see* Hollander, EP:
Principles and methods of social psychology. 2nd ed 1971, p 337).

of doctorates in science and technology awarded in the same years in that
country, which is an indicator of the increase in knowledge. (The bottom
of the curve represents 10,000 and the top 60,000). Grossly oversimplify-
ing, we might say that in any society, there is a category of person who is
concerned with production; another class is concerned with the organisation
of production and distribution of the goods produced by the first category.
There is a third category not directly concerned with any of these things:
into this may be placed the 'thinkers'. As the efficiency of the producers
and organisers increases, the society can then increase the proportion of its
resources devoted to third category persons, including the thinkers who
produce and increase knowledge. (Library school lecturers, as thinkers
about the organisation of the documented thought of the other thinkers,
might be regarded as being at the very end of the chain; as remote as
possible from actual production of useful consumable goods).

Recorded knowledge

One final reason for the growth of knowledge is the ability to record it; that is, the availability of social knowledge as we have defined the term. Without recording, each generation would be able to learn only from the previous generation (or perhaps two); and it would be able to learn only what that generation knew and remembered. Much knowledge would be lost, because it seemed unimportant at the time, even if subsequently it became important. Even more significant, perhaps, is the effect that the availability of social knowledge has on the individual (9a). Particular documents are much more readily available than are particular people, and so it is possible to acquire, through documents, a greater number and variety of ideas than is possible through personal contact, important though personal contact ('informal communication') may be.

The writer's own experience in finding the ideas on which much of this book depends are an example. The documents containing those ideas were readily available to him in a library, and so he was able to add the ideas to his personal knowledge. If, however, it had been necessary, in order to discover those ideas, to rely on meeting the authors of those documents—or even on meeting people who had met them—then it is comparatively unlikely that the ideas would ever have been available. There are about three hundred such authors, none of whom lives near to the writer and most of whom live in places he has never visited: to visit them would in itself constitute a lifetime's work. We can say therefore that social knowledge depends for its increase on the fact that social knowledge exists (3).

The measurement of the growth of knowledge:
units and standards

In order to measure the size, and subsequently the growth, of anything it is necessary to have units or standards of comparison. The growth of children and plants may be measured in centimetres, and it would seem necessary to find or devise a similar unit or standard for knowledge. One unit which suggests itself as a candidate is that used by communications engineers to quantify the amount of information which can be communicated through some channel, such as a telephone line. This unit is the 'bit', short for 'binary digit' (10). If we know that the answer to a question can be only one of two things (such as yes or no) and nothing else (there is no possibility of the answer being 'perhaps'), then the amount of information conveyed by or contained in the answer is one bit. If, for example, the question is 'Is the diameter of Mars greater than the diameter of the

106

Earth?', then the answer (whether it is 'yes' or 'no') contains or conveys one bit of information.

Bits are useful units for the measurement of the length of statements, which is what the communications engineers are concerned with. Unfortunately, they are not an adequate unit for the measurement of what we are concerned with, knowledge and its growth. This can be demonstrated by considering the statement 'Mars is a planet'. This statement contains a definite number of bits of information, the actual number being determined by a calculation involving the number of letters in the English alphabet, their relative frequency of occurrence, and the relative frequency of the occurrence of combinations of them. It implies however a very much larger quantity of *knowledge*, namely all that is known about the properties of planets, and it is impossible to calculate precisely how many bits are involved in the knowledge implied. In a dictionary of science, the implied knowledge might be contained in two or three pages devoted to the entry for planets. At the other extreme, the knowledge implied in the statement is the equivalent of that to be found in a book of two or three hundred pages. Also, a statement made today tells us a great deal more about Mars than was contained in, or implied by, a statement made in 1575 (because of the growth of knowledge about planets). The German statement 'Mars ist ein Planet' contains three more letters and therefore several more bits than the English statement, but both mean the same; they contain exactly equivalent amounts of knowledge. Useful as the bit is as a unit of measurement in engineering, it does not meet our needs for a unit by which knowledge can be quantified. In fact there is not at present any recognised unit by which amounts of knowledge can be measured or quantified exactly. This being the case, it is necessary to find other things which can be measured and which will, in some way, reveal the quantities of knowledge existing at particular times (11). In choosing the things to measure, some care must be taken to ensure that they relate to the same definition of knowledge, and that they always bear the same relationship to that kind of knowledge. Thus, we cannot compare a measurement which relates to the knowledge of an individual, to a measurement which relates to the knowledge of a society. A much smaller proportion of the membership of the Library Association now acquire the status of Fellow than in previous years. This might lead to the conclusion that the knowledge of the average librarian has declined. This would be false, because rather than compare the status levels we should compare the (average) lengths of time required for the education of librarians, in which case the conclusion will be reached that the average new librarian knows much more than his predecessors.

To quantify knowledge and its growth, four possible standards have been suggested: documents, people, institutions and expenditure (12). We can count numbers of documents on the assumption that because these contain knowledge, an increase in their number represents an increase in the quantity of knowledge. We can count the numbers of various categories of people who can be regarded as being concerned with knowledge, such as students, teachers, or research workers. We can also consider the numbers of those who achieve to particular levels of education, assuming that a more highly educated population reflects an increase in the available amount of knowledge. We can also measure the numbers of institutions which are connected with knowledge, such as universities and learned societies. Finally it is possible to examine expenditures on these things, with the assumption that there is a reasonably direct relationship between knowledge and the amount of money spent on it.

Exponential growth

Virtually all of the measurements which relate to the growth of knowledge reveal the same pattern of growth; a pattern which is quite common both in relation to man's other activities, such as his exploitation of natural resources, and in nature, as in the growth of beanstalks on which the first classic discussion of the pattern was based (13).

The pattern has two parts, the first of which corresponds to what is called exponential growth. Table 1 shows the way in which the quantities of something increase when it is undergoing this kind of growth. It will be seen that the number of the period (in column 1) corresponds to the number of times the original quantity is multiplied (column 2). The quantities shown in column 2 can be expressed rather more briefly by using indices or 'exponents' (whence the name), as in column 3, in which it is the exponents which correspond to the number of the period. Column 4 shows the normal method of giving the numbers in columns 2 and 3; in this particular case because the original number was 10, the number of zero digits corresponds to the numbers of the periods in column 1. The original number need not, of course, be 10; it can be any number.

As table 1 shows, exponential growth becomes quite spectacular as it goes on, even if at first it may seem rather slow. The eventual rapidity of exponential growth can be appreciated by starting with two grains of wheat and increasing the quantity exponentially (2^2, 2^3, 2^4, 2^5, . . . , *ie* 4, 8, 16, 32 . . .). If you have sixty-four such

TABLE 1

(1)	(2)	(3)	(4)
Period Period	Number of multiplications	Exponential representation of the numbers	Normal representation of the numbers
1	10	10^1	10
2	10x10	10^2	100
3	10x10x10	10^3	1000
4	10x10x10x10	10^4	10,000
5	10x10x10x10x10	10^5	100,000
6	10x10x10x10x10x10	10^6	1,000,000

increases, the last one will produce enough wheat to cover the whole of England.

The results of measurements of growth are often represented not in tables but in graphs. Figure 2 shows the kind of graph which would represent some of the data in table 1. This kind of graph is not always convenient—apart from anything else, it has a nasty habit of shooting off the top of the paper—and so graphs in the form shown in figure 3 are often used instead. This graph represents the same data. On it, the vertical scale is logarithmic, *ie* it represents the exponents of a number; or, to put it in a more elementary way, the intervals on the vertical scale correspond to the exponents shown in column 3 of table 1. Note that the curve in figure 2 is replaced by a straight line in figure 3: the ability to measure and compare the steepness of such straight lines on logarithmic graphs is another of their advantages.

So far we have used the word 'periods'. These periods could be days, weeks, months, years, or centuries, or anything in between: the choice of period depends entirely on the data and on the convenience of the user of the graph. It is important to appreciate that two things may be growing at *different* rates, but be following the *same* pattern of exponential growth. This of course follows from the previous remark: the periods shown in table 1 might be years or they might be decades; if they are years, the growth must be faster than if they were decades.

Whenever some quantity is increasing on the exponential pattern, it will double not once but frequently: moreover the time taken for each

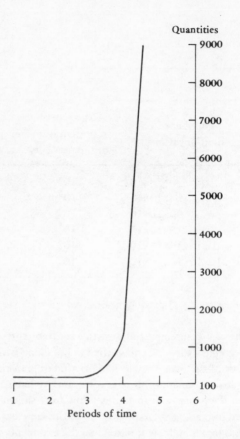

Figure 2: Exponential growth, plotted on normal graph paper

doubling is a constant. That is, the time taken for an increase from 10 to 20 is the same as the time taken for the next doubling, from 20 to 40, and for the next, from 40 to 80, and so on. Because of this constancy, we can use the 'doubling time' as a measure by which to compare two different rates of exponential growth. If the periods in table 1 were years, there is a doubling time of three-tenths of a year; if they were decades, the doubling time would be three years. In relation to knowledge, a doubling time of two and a half years represents very rapid growth, ten to fifteen years is the norm for scientific knowledge, and a doubling time of sixty years would represent very slow growth, suggesting that there was very little interest in the particular kind of knowledge. The faster the growth (and the shorter the doubling time), the steeper will be the line representing it on a logarithmic graph, as shown in figure 4.

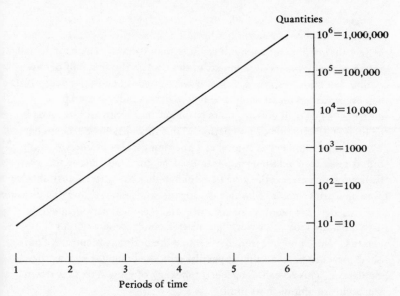

Figure 3: Exponential growth, plotted on logarithmic scale

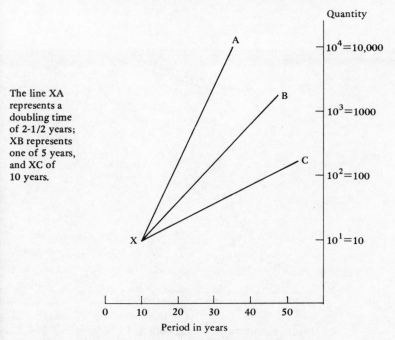

The line XA represents a doubling time of 2-1/2 years; XB represents one of 5 years, and XC of 10 years.

Figure 4: Comparison of different doubling times

Logistic curves

Something very important has been left out of the discussion so far:
the fact that exponential growth cannot go on forever. The exponential
growth of the numbers of scientists in the USA in the first half of this
century means, for example, that if it were to continue to the year 2150,
then every man, woman, child and dog in that country would be a
scientist (14). To all growth, there is a limit; in the case of knowledge,
the limit is usually one of population. Thus there has been an exponential
growth in the numbers of A-level examination passes obtained by sixth-
form (or eighteen year old) pupils in England and Wales and in this case,
the limit which affects the growth is the number of eighteen year olds in
those countries. Figure 5, which is a logarithmic graph, shows one measure
of knowledge, the numbers of scientific and technical periodicals compared with the growth of world population, and is generally representative. Note how the line representing the periodicals currently published curves to become almost parallel with the line representing the
population. This reveals the general tendency of growth to slow down
as it begins to approach its limit.

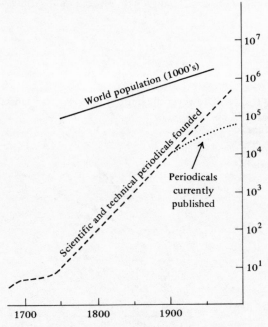

Figure 5: Comparison of growth of knowledge
with growth of population

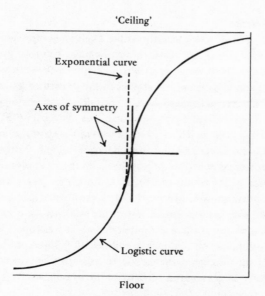

Figure 6: Logistic growth

Figure 6 represents the idealised case of growth as affected by some limiting factor, or 'ceiling' plotted on a normal arithmetic graph. The curve which represents growth is called a logistic, or s-curve. In this graph the limit is constant, and may be referred to as the 'saturation point'. In many real cases however the limit or ceiling is not constant and is itself increasing, as in the case of world population shown in figure 5. Another noticeable feature of figure 6 is the way in which the curve can be divided into two, mirror-image, halves which meet where the 'axes of symmetry' cross over: this is the point where half of the growth has taken place and half of the time has elapsed.

Exponential growth (as shown in table 1 and figures 2 and 3) is really only half the picture (strictly, slightly less than half). It only continues when, and as long as, the limiting factor on growth has not begun to affect it; when the limiting factor begins to take effect, growth follows the logistic curve pattern of figure 6, slowing down until it has stopped or virtually done so. The pattern in figure 6 is, of course, an ideal one; real measurements may diverge from it, particularly as the limit of growth is approached, when the curve usually begins to wobble in various ways. Sometimes it looks like a staircase (or 'escalates'). The suggestion has been made that growth does not 'enjoy' being limited, and tries to push its ceiling up.

Measurements

In a book of this size it is not possible to give a comprehensive set of all the kinds of measurement which may be made to prove the thesis that the pattern of growth which applies to so many things—the pattern of exponential and logistic curves—applies to the growth of knowledge. Nor indeed is it necessary, because there is considerable literature on the subject, much of which is likely to be available to the reader (15). In any case, the best way in which to be convinced of the existence of exponential growth is to collect and plot some data for oneself. Many of the writer's students have had to do just that, and the examples which follow are a selection of the results obtained. Although the items which have been selected are those which most clearly show the expected pattern, it is true to say that in every case in which the students were able to collect data, some approximation to exponential growth was found, even in the case of British books on the reading abilities of children, the total number of which, at the time when the data were collected, was twenty-five. It is hoped that the subject matter of most of the examples will give them added relevance (7).

Figures 7-9 all show exponential growth. Figure 7 relates to the literature of librarianship and is based on two independent data collections. It does not, incidentally, take into account periodicals which have ceased

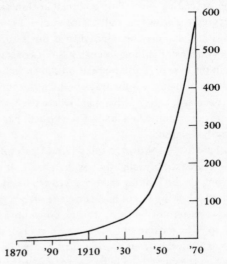

Figure 7: Numbers of librarianship periodicals, 1876-1970
(Source: Ulrich's *Directory of periodicals*)
114

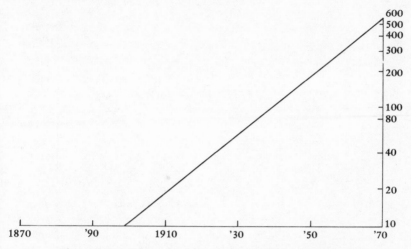

Figure 8: Data from figure 7, plotted with logarithmic scale

publication. It may be noted that the first date of publication of a periodical devoted to librarianship was 1876: this is one basis of the earlier
claim that the profession is about a century old.

Figure 8 is based on the same data and is included to show, in a real
case, the effect of using a logarithmic scale: the curve is replaced by a
straight line.

Figure 9 also uses a logarithmic scale, although the straight line is
not quite so clear. Interestingly, the doubling time represented by the
dashed line which joins the two ends of the slope is 12·5 years—which
is in the middle of the 10-15 year range found by Price for science and
technology. The doubling time in the period 1930-1940, when growth
seems to have been fastest, is 7·5 years; if this had been maintained, the
membership of the Library Association in 1975 would have been in the
region of 120,000, compared with the actual figure of less than 25,000.

Figures 10 and 11 may be considered together. It should be mentioned that the waviness of the curve in figure 10 until about 1960 is,
or may be, due to the inaccuracy of the statistics on which the graphs
are based. Certainly the figures for the library school in Newcastle
turned out to be widely at variance with the memories of those who
were there at that time. Part of the inconsistency is due, no doubt, to
the large numbers of part-time and visiting lecturers on whom the schools
relied in the past. In both cases growth is limited by the fact that the
schools ought not to produce more librarians than there are jobs available,

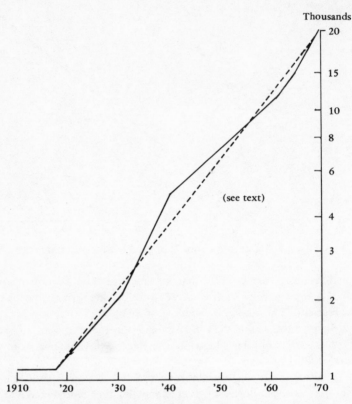

Figure 9: Numbers of personal members of the Library Association
(plotted on a logarithmic scale)
(Source: Library Association Yearbooks)

as their courses are (or have been) directed to providing an education for the profession of librarianship, as opposed to courses in English or history, which are usually regarded as general education.

This fact, and its relevance, have been forced upon the attention of the library schools by the Department of Education and Science, which has limited the number of students they may take in at any one time. The logistic curve drawn on figure 11 seems to fit the actual statistics rather nicely. The big drop in the numbers of students in the years prior to 1970 almost certainly reflects the fact that it was about this time that the schools began to introduce three-year degree courses, which have largely replaced the two-year professional courses, previously their main concern. The corresponding bend in the lecturers' curve presumably arises from the same cause.

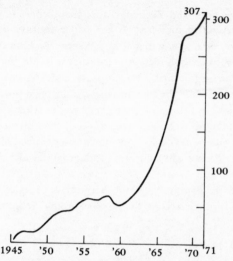

Figure 10: Numbers of lecturers in British library schools
(excluding University College, London)

(Source: Library Association Yearbooks. The figures are affected by differing
methods of counting part-time and visiting lecturers in the period to 1965).

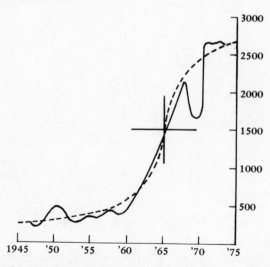

Figure 11: Numbers of librarianship students in Great Britain

(Sources: Bradley, D. *Development of full time education for librarianship
since the war* (thesis, 1968); and elsewhere. The dashed line represents a
logistic curve, whose axes of symmetry are also shown.)

Earlier we remarked on the fact that growth does not appear to enjoy being subjected to limitations. In this particular case, education for librarianship, we may say that although there is a limit on the amount of librarians the schools may produce, they are able, within other limits, to extend the length of time taken for the education of librarians— thus, within a decade the time has increased from a norm of one year's full time study to a norm of three years' study. This is put forward only as an example of how growth reacts to the presence of limits, and not for the sake of making any comment on the need for the increased length of time. It might well have produced an escalating curve in figure 11.

Of all the diagrams referred to, that in figure 12 gives the clearest vindication for the assertion that growth of knowledge tends to follow

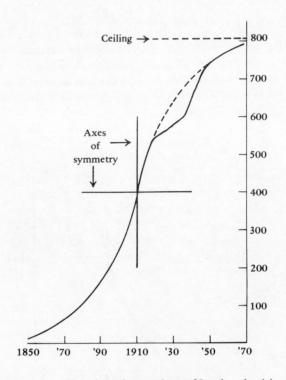

Figure 12: Growth in the numbers of local authorities
having adopted the Public Libraries Acts

(Because of subsequent amalgamations.the total number of library authorities
was rather smaller than the numbers indicated.)

a logistic pattern. It was expected that the data for the growth of public libraries in Britain would show something approximating to that pattern. It was known that there was a ceiling—the number of local government authorities which were empowered to be library authorities—and, moreover, that the ceiling had been reached, since everyone in Britain now lives within the boundaries of a library authority. (Note that this diagram refers to the situation prior to the reorganisation of local government in Britain.) What was remarkable, therefore, about the outcome of the plot of the data was not that an approximation to a logistic curve appeared, but that it was such a close approximation; the closest, in fact, that the writer has ever seen for data relating to the growth of knowledge.

Conclusions and summary

In the introduction to this chapter it was claimed that it is obvious that knowledge grows. Various reasons for this have been suggested: the need for knowledge; human curiosity; the fact that there are more people to know (and be curious about) things; increasing specialisation resulting from man's habit of tending to live in larger and larger communities; the increased efficiency of production which enables a society to employ fewer and fewer people to produce the necessities of life, allowing a larger proportion to do things like write about the nature of knowledge; and, finally, the existence of recorded knowledge itself, which allows people to have increased access to the knowledge that already exists.

There is no unit for the measurement of knowledge itself, and so other criteria have to be used, such as the numbers of documents, of people and institutions concerned with knowledge, and the amounts of money spent on these things. The general pattern of growth, and various terms and ideas used in connection with its measurement, such as exponential growth and logistic curves, have been discussed.

Finally, we have examined some of the data relating to libraries and librarianship. These have generally confirmed the claim that knowledge grows, and that this growth conforms to the exponential/logistic pattern. Of course, to agree with this statement, it is necessary to agree that numbers of librarianship periodicals, of librarians, of library school lecturers and students indicate the growth of knowledge on the subject.

Some of the figures suggest that the increase in knowledge is slowing down. It is certainly true that the growth of public librarianship in Britain has reached its limit: everyone in Britain is now, at least nominally (and generally in fact), served by a public library. This still, of course, leaves room for expansion, even within the public library service (for example in the provision of new and better branch libraries, and of such

119

services as those to house-bound readers); and there are numerous other, non-public, library services which could be developed, particularly those connected with educational establishments. Moreover, on the world scale there is still considerable room for expansion (for example, France has one library schoool, compared with the sixteen in Britain); and elsewhere, some of this expansion is taking place (Australia has recently created a number of library schools).

More generally it is true that in some fields and places the growth of knowledge does show definite signs of slowing down, as data for physics and chemistry in the USA (figure 13) suggest (16). This is probably not true for knowledge as a whole, but rather indicative of a shift of interest from one area of knowledge to others, a contention borne out by figure 14.

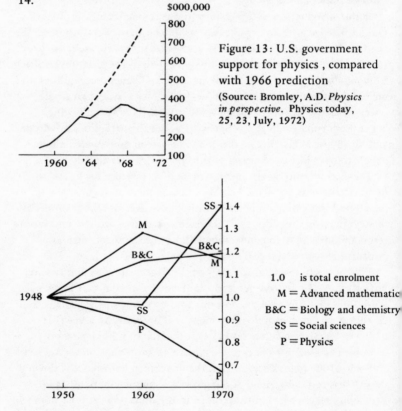

Figure 13: U.S. government support for physics , compared with 1966 prediction
(Source: Bromley, A.D. *Physics in perspective*. Physics today, 25, 23, July, 1972)

1.0   is total enrolment
M = Advanced mathematic
B&C = Biology and chemistry
SS = Social sciences
P = Physics

Figure 14: Choice of subjects among pupils in US high schools
Source: Bromley, A.D. *Physics in perspective*. Physics today, 25, 23, July 1972.

Quite apart from the USA (and other developed countries), there are, of course, many other countries in which the impact of the exponential growth of knowledge is only now beginning to be felt, as might be revealed by an examination of statistics for universities in Africa and the Middle East. The conclusion is that knowledge does increase, even if the support for, and interest in, some particular kinds of knowledge in some particular places has waned.

NOTES AND REFERENCES

1 Price (1963) will be particularly useful to the reader of this chapter; it, and Machlup (1962) are classics. Meadows (1974) and Menard (1971), although restricted to science, also are useful introductions to the subject. Rider (1944) was probably the first work to draw the attention of librarians to this topic and its importance.

2 See chapter 1, note 1, especially Platt (1959). For sensory deprivation see Lindsay (1972) p 620-622.

3 See also Toffler (1970) p 30-32, which deals with 'knowledge as fuel for change'.

4 Beaujeu-Garnier (1966) ch 7; Clark (1967); Cox (1970) ch 19 and 20; Mack (1973) ch 9 and 10; Sampson (1971) p 420ff.

5 Bell (1966) and Sheldon (1968) contain long detailed discussions and data.

6 Mack (1973) ch 3 deals with differentiation. See also Price (1975) p 119. For a possible further explanation, see Harmon (1973).

7 Bramley (1969).

8 A more detailed account of the ideas is given in Ranganathan (1967), Part P.

9 White (1959) p 298-300; Darlington (1969); also Adams (1960) on the evolution of cities; Mack (1973) and Sampson (1971) as note 4.

9a See also Riesman (1970).

10 Mackay (1969) and Cherry (1966) both contain readable accounts, but almost any elementary text on communications engineering will have one.

11 See also Holton (1962).

12 Machlup (1962).

13 Price (1963) ch 1. Richman (1973) is a clear account of the mathematical ideas involved, recommended to even the most anti-numerate.

14 Compare Boulding (1970).

15 Price (1963), Machlup (1972), Meadows (1974) and Menard (1971) are all useful (see note 1); also Sheldon (1968). Anthony (1969a), Gottschalk (1963), Urquhart (1964) and Vickery (1968) contain data, believed

reliable, for science and technology. Anthony (1969b) is an example of the many specialist investigations.

16 On stability and equilibria in knowledge, see Kochen (1969), which has a good bibliography.   See also Price (1975) p 118-119, and Boulding (1970).

Chapter 9

GROWTH OF KNOWLEDGE, II:
COMMENTS AND IMPLICATIONS

INTRODUCTION: In this chapter, we discuss the process by which the increase of knowledge is brought about, and examine its effects on knowledge itself, and its implications for the individual and for libraries (1). We are here especially concerned with social knowledge, although a comparison is made with personal knowledge. In this discussion it is necessary to consider the point that there may be more than one kind of social knowledge, although the full discussion of the matter is the subject of the next chapter. We also comment on and attempt to counter criticisms which have been made of the use of counts of numbers of documents as criteria for the measurement of the increase in knowledge.

Growth, not increase
The conclusion of the previous chapter was that the amount of knowledge has increased and is likely to increase. Consideration of the ideas of Public Knowledge, consensus, and World Three suggests, however, that the word 'growth', as used in the chapter titles, is much more appropriate than the word 'increase'. If there was mere increase, new items of knowledge would simply be added to a pile of existing knowledge without there being any effect on the totality of knowledge or on individual items within it.

It is obvious that the increase in knowledge is not like that. In the first place, new knowledge is dependent on previously existing knowledge. Reverting to our potato plant example, it might be that a second scientist finds that some ash does not improve the growth of potato plants: this is a 'problem' which may be solved by another scientist who discovers that it must be wood ash. Subsequently another scientist may identify a particular chemical present in wood ash which appears responsible for the improved growth, and that otherwise ash has no effect. It would not have been possible (or, at least, highly unlikely) that this idea could have been realised without the original observation and hypothesis of our original potato plant scientist.

Secondly, this new knowledge is incorporated into the consensus. It affects the concepts of the potato plant scientists concerned, it is connected to earlier knowledge by the process of self-organisation already described (p 79), and by its assimilation into the literature (see table 1).

Thirdly, the consensus is changed. At first it was that ashy soils improve the growth of potato plants, then the consensus was that *some* ashy soil had the effect (but which and why was not known), and ultimately the consensus becomes that some particular chemical which can be added to the soil is responsible and that ash itself it not important. (Simultaneously, the consensus may have been changed in other ways, by involving other plants, by defining the idea of 'good growth', and eventually by identifying different chemicals for different plants.)

Knowledge *grows* by a cumulative process in which new knowledge is dependent upon that already in existence and in which new knowledge is gradually accumulated. Thus the consensus is gradually changed until eventually it is radically different from the form it had when the process was begun. Knowledge cumulates, and as it cumulates it changes. We may note here the analogy which exists between this cumulative process in the growth of social knowledge, and the processes involved in conceptualisation, especially in the case of adults (p 50). Conceptualisation, or learning, involves changing, modifying, extending and reorganising existing concepts, rather than the creation of completely new ones (2).

The notion of change may be put in an educational context: the 'correct answer' to examination questions is often (but not always) that which most precisely represents the consensus. Students at one stage might get full marks for writing that potato plants grow better in ashy soil; but their successors may have to mention particular plants and particular chemicals for each, among other things. The story is told of a professor who was taxed with the fact that year after year the same question appeared in the examination papers which he set; to which he replied that the question might be the same but the answers were always different.

Knowledge as a system

The ideas of change and assimilation mentioned earlier provide the starting point for an analogy between knowledge as a system and a living organism as a system (3). The input to the knowledge system is data; the input to the organism is food. Animals do not grow by simply

124

PUBLICATION FORMAT	AUDIENCE TO WHOM KNOWLEDGE WILL BECOME AVAILABLE
1 Issue of draft or preprint to author's specialist friends, acquaintances and colleagues (informal communication)	Author's specialist friends, acquaintances and colleagues (and their friends, acquaintances and colleagues)
2 Publication in a specialist periodical	All or most specialists in the subject
3 Re-publication in another specialist journal, issue of reprint	Members of other specialist groups, specialists who did not see the original publication
4 Issue in special format, *eg* report, patent	Further specialists
5 Re-writing and publication in another version	Another group of specialists, probably very different from any of the groups above
6 Re-presentation, di cussion and criticisms in revie⸍ /s, usually aimed at specialists and written by another author	A rather wider and less specialised group. The process of integration into the consensus begins at this stage
7 Translation	Readers of another language
8 Re-presentation in monograph by same or another author	Specialists in the same or other fields: incorporated into this format, the idea is likely to be widely available for some time
9 Textbook (at different levels)	Students (at different levels)
10 Popular book	Laymen: non-specialists in general
11 Children's book	Children
12 Educational medium, *eg* film, video-tape	Students, schoolchildren
13 Radio and television programmes	Mass audience of laymen. The programmes may be recorded and used in educational contexts: or their content may be re-issued in printed format, as Magee (1971) and Cooke (1974) in the bibliography

Table 1: Publications and their audiences

The formats are in the approximate sequence in which they might occur to an item of knowledge which eventually becomes 'embedded' into the consensus, although a different sequence may occur; probably in about 50% of cases there is only one occasion when an item is published, and it does not enter the consensus.

sticking lumps of raw food onto themselves, but by digesting and assimilating its useful constituents for growth and living (and discarding those which they do not need); so too the input data to the knowledge system are not just stuck onto the existing knowledge, but are analysed and their components sorted, correlated and compared, and, if useful, they serve to enlarge 'the body of knowledge' or practical technological purposes.

The systems view of knowledge is an important one which both suggests and confirms various properties of knowledge, such as organisation, growth, and increasing complexity and differentiation, all of which we discuss.

It has been suggested that the gradual process of cumulation and that of 'revolution', which is our next topic, are too random and haphazard to account for the organisation and orderliness of the knowledge system; some additional process is required (4). It may well be that this is provided by the fact that science—and other bodies of knowledge—result from social processes, rather than from the efforts of random individuals, as suggested by Ziman (4a).

An additional property of systems is that they eventually reach a stage at which they become stable, and they expend energy to maintain this stability. This is technically referred to as homeostasis, and the idea is discussed in relation to knowledge by Kochen (5).

Scientific revolutions

Another very important notion is that the gradual process of the growth of knowledge does not always occur (although it is the normal pattern); sometimes there are 'revolutions' which completely overthrow existing knowledge. In our example there was at one stage a problem—why does some ashy soil not affect the growth of plants? This was 'solved' by the discovery of a new 'idea' which improved, or refined, the old one, by specifying the kind of ash. Then there was another problem—why only wood ash? This in its turn was solved by discovering that there was a particular chemical involved. These problems were both solved within the same general framework of knowledge as had previously existed, namely that the nature of the soil in which plants grow affects their growth. Such frameworks are referred to in the present context as 'paradigms'.

Sometimes, however, a problem, or more likely several problems, occur which cannot be dealt with in this way. It may happen, for instance, that the data acquired as a result of tests all appear to falsify the ideas in the consensus, and that there is no way in which the consensus can be improved or refined to account for them. When this happens it may eventually prove necessary to find a solution, or idea, which completely changes the existing paradigm. Our potato example is at last exhausted, and instead two actual examples are given.

126

The classic case is often referred to as the Copernican Revolution. In the early fifteenth century the paradigm of the structure of the heavens was that the Earth was at the centre of the Universe and that all the moving heavenly bodies—the Sun, the Moon, and the planets—revolved around the Earth. It was also part of the paradigm that 'perfect' motion was circular. As numerous and more accurate observations became available, the data could not easily be fitted into this paradigm. A 'revolution' took place, and when it was complete, the paradigm had been altered in its entirety: the Sun was the centre around which the planets moved, and their motion was no longer circular but elliptical (6).

Another contemporary revolution relates to the position of the continents. Twenty years ago, the paradigm was that the present positions of the continents were the positions in which they had always been. Although it had been noted that there were certain curious similarities in the shapes of the continents, notably the way in which the shape of the South American continent fits into the shape of Africa (a fit which is even closer when the continental shelves rather than the land areas themselves are compared), and although one man (Wegener) had hypothesised that the continents had moved relative to each other, this had not affected the paradigm, as there was no known force on the Earth large enough to move the continents about. Within the space of about five years, not only had such a force been discovered, but there were several instances of the effect it had. And so, in that short space of time a completely new paradigm, involving the movements of the continents, was adopted by the scientists concerned (7).

We should note that, in both cases, the old paradigm was accepted because it was reasonable to accept it. It was, in Popper's term, credible, in the sense that it agreed with what was known, and therefore it was, as Ziman would express it, (part of) the consensus. In both cases, the new paradigm was adopted because it was a better explanation of new data which became available and which did not fit into the old paradigm. The old paradigm became, because of the new data, completely incredible.

The idea of scientific revolutions has been argued forcibly by Kuhn, who makes a clear distinction between normal science and revolutionary science (8). In normal science, the work of the scientists involved is concerned with filling out the details of a paradigm, *eg* by identifying which substances in the soil improve the growth of individual kinds of plants. Revolution in science, by contrast, occurs when a new or different paradigm (or consensus) is created. Science can be thought of as an attempt to create a picture or model of the universe. When a model of a house is made from toy bricks, bricks can be added to make the model more and more realistic; this is quite a normal procedure, involving improvements rather than radical changes. If, however, the model maker is left with many unused bricks, some of which are awkwardly shaped so that they cannot easily be fitted into the existing model (like data which cannot be fitted or assimilated into an existing paradigm), then the only way to use them to build an even more realistic model is to scrap the existing model and begin again. This is what happens in revolutionary science. (We might note that the boundary between revolutionary and normal science is not perhaps always quite as clear: sometimes changes are made to the paradigm which are fundamental, but which do not involve altering it completely).

It seems that, so far as scientific knowledge is concerned, it is changing, either gradually and continually by the normal process of cumulation, or else suddenly and more radically in more or less revolutionary changes. Knowledge, then, is unlike the laws of the Medes and the Persians ('which altereth not'): knowledge changes.

Non-scientific knowledge and cumulation

The idea that knowledge 'grows' by a process of cumulation is based on the observation of how scientific knowledge develops, or is developed. The suggestion is sometimes made, however, that not all knowledge is like this; that some knowledge is non-cumulative, and indeed cannot be cumulative by its very nature (9). Although we shall discuss the possibility of the existence of different kinds of knowledge in the next chapter, it is appropriate to examine this particular point here.

Undoubtedly some knowledge, not usually regarded as scientific, is cumulative. For example, the hypothesis that there is a relation between the environment in which a society lives, the language it uses, and the way in which its members think, depends on cumulated evidence; and when a sociologist or anthropologist visits a previously unobserved community in order to investigate these matters, the knowledge he acquires depends on that hypothesis and will improve and refine it in a cumulative manner. In some cases the notion of cumulation is more difficult to justify, because the relationship between new and previously existing knowledge is less easily seen than in science. Nevertheless, the new ideas show the influence of previous ones, even if they are different from them, and so there is a gradual change in knowledge. We could use the word 'evolution' for such instances. Evolution takes place in many kinds of knowledge, even in such things as knowledge of ethics, which might be thought of as

128

constant and absolute. Evidence for this can be found in Biblical studies (as witness the evolution from ideas such as 'an eye for an eye' into ideas like 'blessed are the meek').

It is, however, particularly in relation to the humanities, the arts and literature, that the idea of non-cumulativeness is put forward. It is sometimes suggested that these are 'additive' rather than cumulative, and they are, therefore, not subject to change.(10). Two counter-arguments, based partly on the ideas presented in previous chapters, suggest themselves. The first relates to techniques: the techniques available to artists have been improved and extended, partly as the result of technological developments, as (obviously) in the case of television and films, and also (perhaps less obviously) in the case of the novel, which is dependent on the invention of printing. Not all of the changes in techniques have depended on technology. Consider the very ancient art form of sculpture. The results of Epstein's use of techniques in many cases would have been as much appreciated by Greek sculptors as they are at the present time. On the other hand it is doubtful whether the Greeks would have been able to see the qualities of the abstract works of Henry Moore. There has been a change in sculpture, and arguably the change has come about by a process of evolution if not of cumulation. Such a discussion of techniques might be dismissed as irrelevant and facile: it might be pointed out that it is not the techniques themselves which are subject to change, but it is the ideas which those techniques are used to express which are non-cumulative.

Our second counter-argument against this notion has three parts. Firstly, the ideas which an artist tries to convey are largely (though not of course entirely) those accepted in the society in which he lives, or in some part of it. To give just one example, the plays of Shaw may be considered to represent not just his own ideas, but the ideas of the social reformers of his day. The second part of the argument is that knowledge is different in different societies, and that this difference must affect the ideas of the artists as much as it affects the ideas of others. The art of the Greek sculptors, of Michelangelo and of Epstein cannot be attempts to present the same ideas because the ideas of the societies in which they lived were so different. The third part is to point out that modern western civilisation is influenced by, and, in part, evolved from renaissance Italy; similarly renaissance Italy was much influenced by Greek culture.

It may well be that there are two kinds of knowledge; but to suggest that to distinguish between them, on the grounds that one is subject to continual change while the other is changeless, is probably not the best way of making the distinction. The ideas of artists, and the ways in which

129

they try to express them are both subject to evolution (if not cumulation) and change.

World Three, Public Knowledge, and growth

In our discussion so far, the tendency has been to regard Popper's concept of World Three, Ziman's ideas about Public Knowledge and the consensus, and the idea of paradigms as being more or less the same and also as being sufficiently similar to what we have defined as the meaning of 'social knowledge' for it to be possible to assume that what was true for one of these was true for them all, and true in particular for social knowledge. In connection with the idea of growth, however, this is—or may be—an invalid assumption. The notions of Public Knowledge and the consensus, and of paradigms, are all taken from writings concerned with scientific knowledge, although Ziman has suggested that his ideas may apply to at least some other kinds of knowledge also. In describing Popper's World Three, Magee has by contrast referred to it as 'the whole cultural heritage' (11) so that it must contain not only scientific knowledge, but also the humanities knowledge to which we referred in the previous section.

World Three and Public Knowledge both relate to documents: in both cases the existence of documents is essential. Their relationships to documents are however significantly different, particularly and in a very practical way, for librarians. A document is part of Public Knowledge only as long as the majority of statements contained therein are in agreement with the *current* consensus (or discuss its falsification). When the statements no longer relate to the current consensus in these ways, because the consensus has changed, the document is no longer part of Public Knowledge. This happens even though *some* of the statements are still part of the consensus. Thus Newton's *Principia mathematica* contains statements which are still part of the consensus, even though the document itself is no longer part of Public Knowledge. The result is that, generally, in order to have the current consensus, or Public Knowledge, available, it is necessary only to have recent documents available. Even if some part of the consensus originated many years ago, it will not be necessary to have access to the document in which it first appeared, because the idea will be repeated in more recent documents. Thus it is claimed that if all scientific documents more than twenty years old were to be destroyed, the effect on science would be negligible. (It should be pointed out that in certain specific instances, and in certain kinds of science, the twenty year period would be too short: nevertheless, the general argument still holds true).

130

The same claim is not, however, true for the relationship between World Three and documents: if all the copies of Shakespeare's plays, for example, were to be destroyed, this would affect the 'cultural heritage': World Three would be diminished. This obviously reflects the difference, postulated previously, between knowledge in the humanities and knowledge of the sciences. Nevertheless, it is also true that the *Principia mathematica* is also part of our cultural heritage, and destruction of all copies of that work (which would not, as was described, affect Public Knowledge) would affect our cultural heritage. In order to have access to the cultural heritage, it is necessary to have access to *all* documents.

Social knowledge is knowledge available in the form of documents. If we equate social knowledge with Public Knowledge, there are fewer documents than if we equate social knowledge with World Three.

Implications of growth

In this and the previous chapter, we have demonstrated that knowledge increases exponentially in quantity, and that much of the increase results from a process of cumulative growth, which involves change. There are a number of consequences of these ideas, both for the individual as a 'consumer' of knowledge, and for the nature of social knowledge.

Too much knowledge

The first implication for the individual is that there is too much social knowledge available for him as an individual to know it all. This has not always been the case: certain Greeks, some of the mediaeval encyclopaedists and other more recent polymaths could justifiably claim that they had expert knowledge over the whole range of human wisdom, being equally at home with works of literature and the arts, with the sciences of all kinds, and with history, politics and economics. But no person could now reasonably claim that he is equally expert on all these things: there are those like C P Snow who are justly given credit for their abilities in different fields, but this does not mean that they would claim to be an expert in all fields. No matter how intelligent the person is, there is not enough time in a single human life to be able to absorb the total contents of all social knowledge.

The stage has been reached where it is now difficult not merely to find out what one wants to know, but even to find out whether such knowledge actually exists. Sometimes, in the case of science and technology, it has become cheaper to conduct an experiment to find something out, rather than to attempt to discover whether the experiment has previously been performed. The situation has been accurately described by Thurber (12): 'So much has been written about everything, that you can't find out anything about it'.

Too much new knowledge

The second result relates, not to the amount of existing knowledge, but to the amount of new knowledge which constantly becomes available. There is too much new knowledge for the individual to be able to cope with it all. This is sometimes referred to as 'information overload' (13). As an example, a calculation for one of the branches of science showed that if the scientist were to attempt to keep up with all the new literature on the subject and were to devote *all* his time to the task, he would find that after two months of hard work, he would already be six weeks behind in his reading. Some years ago, an article on information retrieval was given the title 'Of needles and haystacks'. Looking for information is not just looking for needles in a haystack—it is like looking for needles in a haystack onto which more and more hay, some with needles in it, is being continually thrown.

Specialisation

The problem of information overload has several solutions (13), but we shall refer to only one of them—the solution of increased specialisation. Here the individual concentrates on some particular aspect of his subject, and learns more and more about that, but, at the same time, becomes increasingly unaware of the current state of knowledge in those parts of the subject not relating to the aspect on which he is concentrating. Increasing specialisation brings with it, however, its own problems which affect both the individual, and as we shall see later, the structure of recorded social knowledge. One of these problems is that each individual specialisation tends to develop its own special language, or jargon, with the intention of facilitating communication between the specialists. This results in what has been dubbed the 'Law of mutual incomprehension'— the fact that it becomes increasingly difficult for a specialist in one area to communicate with a specialist in another area (14). The original contributors to library mechanisation, for example, were naturally experts *either* in librarianship *or* in the use of computers, and the two groups found that although they used the same sets of words, including terms such as 'index' and 'format', they used them to refer to different things. This had all sorts of consequences, some of which were amusing but most of which were inconvenient. We should note in this connection the general tendency to use normal words with special meanings ('cradle' has seven different meanings each used in a different technology); the invention of new words and the use of abbreviations ('telex', 'television', 'telecast', CCTV, VDU).

Language

The problem of language is a fact of major importance in relation to social knowledge. It is possible to ascribe the problem, at least in part, to the growth of knowledge; because the growth has involved a spread of knowledge, but it would not be reasonable to advance this as the whole cause. Without examining this point further, we shall simply say that knowledge is an international commodity which crosses national and linguistic boundaries. For this purpose, translations are necessary, which is an instance of the redundancy which we shall describe later (p 136), and adds a further row to table 1.

Further, the effect of the relation between language, thought and knowledge, which we discussed at some length in chapter 7, may be to make translation difficult and sometimes even impossible. Chinese, for example, does not have a word for 'love'; United Nations interpreters also found great difficulty in devising a word in that language which would translate the name of the metal uranium. As another example, we discussed the meaning of 'I know' in chapter 4; a Frenchman discussing the same idea would have to begin by concerning himself not only with 'je sais' but also with 'je connais' (15).

Social knowledge

The fact that social knowledge grows has the obvious implication of there being more documents, which creates for libraries the problem of storage—where to put them all (16). This problem is acute for those libraries, such as national libraries, concerned with social knowledge in Popper's World Three, ('entire cultural heritage') sense, and which, therefore, collect and preserve all documents. But it also (because of the exponential increase) affects even those libraries whose policy is based entirely on the Public Knowledge, (consensus) view of social knowledge, and which discard the documents no longer relating to the consensus.

For many libraries the growth of available social knowledge outstrips the resources (of finance and space) available to them. This increases the need to select the documents to be added to their libraries, and makes the actual choice more difficult. An effect of the growth of technological

133

knowledge is that there is an increasing number of different *kinds* of documents which libraries are expected to make available; this adds to the problems both of selection and storage. On the other hand, technology provides at least some partial solutions, such as microcopies and photocopies, and the ability of the computer to provide assistance in the handling and organisation of document references (17, 17a).

Change and complexity

Numerous references have been made to the fact that as social knowledge grows, it changes: in discussing the idea of specialisation as a *cause* of growth, we referred to the ideas of fission and fusion.

It is now necessary to point out that specialisation is not only a cause of the growth of knowledge, it is also one of its consequences. There are now people who specialise in being generalists, as in the Royal College of *General* Practitioners. Specialisation in social knowledge is, of course, a reflection of the specialisation which is adopted by individuals to overcome their particular problems resulting from the growth of knowledge. Indeed it has been suggested that new 'disciplines' arise because of the limited memory spans which affect personal knowledge (18).

Fission was described as a process whereby a single specialisation breaks down into a number of narrower specialisations. Obviously, this involves change, but this change only affects the specialisation and does not alter the general pattern—the overall structure—of knowledge. Growth by fusion, however, is another matter altogether, because the new specialisations have many parents. As this process of fusion occurs, it creates the problem that the relationships between different areas of knowledge become increasingly complex. Thus, recalling a previous example, we might have the two parents of computer science and librarianship fusing to form the subject of library mechanisation: computer science is a good example because it has this kind of relationship not only with librarianship, but with all other branches of human endeavour in which computers have been used.

Not only do the relationships become increasingly complex, however, they, like the individual areas of knowledge themselves, change. Thus the misuse of alcohol may perhaps be regarded initally as a problem within religious ethics, then as a more general ethical problem, and subsequently it may be seen as a disease. Another example, referred to both earlier and later, is psychology. One hundred years ago it was a branch of philosophy but now belongs to the sciences, and has connections with the social sciences (19). There is also a whole series of complex and changing relationships between the 'pure' sciences and the technologies which are more or less closely related to them.

In sum, it is not merely the case that social knowledge increases, because it in fact *grows*; and it is not merely that it grows, because as it grows it becomes more complex and the relationships between its components change. In all of this, it reveals its system-like properties.

Increase in document numbers or growth of knowledge?

Before we leave the question of the growth of knowledge, one final point remains to be discussed. When the means whereby the growth of knowledge were examined, it was pointed out that numbers of documents could be used as a criterion, and we gave an example. An objection to this method has been raised, however, and we can now consider it (20).

The objection is that the amount of publication—the quantities of documents—is not necessarily a good indicator of the amount of knowledge available, simply because there is a great deal of duplicate publication, so that, so far as making knowledge available is concerned, much of the publication is unnecessary; many publications, in fact, do not contain any new knowledge but merely repeat what is already available elsewhere. The quantity of new knowledge is therefore much less than the amount of new documents would seem to indicate.

There can be no doubt that in the case of science and technology, the same text is often issued not once but several times. An article in a scientific periodical, for instance, may as a matter of course also be issued in 'preprint' form immediately after it is written and prior to publication, and subsequently re-issued as a reprint. Commonly too (at least at the time when the writer was dealing with such literature) the same text would appear as a report from a government laboratory. The record within his experience was one particular item, a paper presented by an American scientist at a conference in Scandinavia, which was received as part of three different series in his library, and which he noted from the abstract journals had also been issued in four other formats. This is (one might hope) the extreme example of 'direct duplication', and duplication to this extent is difficult to justify.

Much of the so-called duplication does not, however, take the form of the straightforward unaltered duplication of a text, but rather it is a matter of re-presentation of an item of knowledge (2). In table 1 an indication is given of the various ways in which an item of knowledge might be 're-presented', and against each of them is shown the 'audience' or potential readership which it would reach. The important feature which we have tried to show in the table is how each successive re-presentation of the item makes it available to a wider or a different audience; at each stage the idea is communicated to more people.

Assimilation and redundancy

Is all this re-presentation of the same item of knowledge to be regarded as duplication? Does it mean that the numbers of documents do not accurately reflect the growth of knowledge? Is it wasteful? It is suggested that the answer to all these questions is 'no'—or at least, not entirely. Ther are at least two reasons for this claim. The first is that in many, if not all, of the re-presentations of the item of knowledge, it is being assimilated into the consensus: its relationship to other items of knowledge is being discussed, evaluated, and accepted (or, at some stages, it is being rejected, in which case it will not arrive at the final stage). We might in fact say that it is being 'organised' into the consensus—a point to which we shortly return.

The second reason is based on the idea (from communications theory) of 'redundancy'. In this context, redundancy is not something which is essentially useless and wasteful—it is feature of a great deal of human communication. (As an example, we might say that 'rain is drops of water falling from clouds in the sky'. The last three words are redundant, because where else would we find clouds? But in this case, those words help the listener to realise that we did say 'clouds', and not 'crowds'). One common form of redundancy is repetition (or duplication): this too can help the audience to get the message correctly.

In the case of the re-presentation of the same item of knowledge over and over again in documents of different sorts, the redundancy takes the form of repeating the message for a different audience (just as a politician may repeat the same speech to different audiences in different parts of his constituency). The reason why it is considered that this redundancy reflects the growth of knowledge is that it is because of the growth of knowledge that so many different audiences may exist for the same item of knowledge. If knowledge did not grow, there would be no specialisation, and without specialisation, there would be no specialists to form different audiences for the same item of knowledge. Also there would not exist different *levels* of specialisation, as exemplified in the table by specialists, students, laymen, and schoolchildren. (The table could have been elaborated to show also the existence of different degrees of specialisation among the specialists themselves.)

In other words, the contention is that while the numbers of documents may not be directly related to the growth of knowledge, because many documents repeat or re-present existing items of knowledge rather than put forward new items, those numbers do reflect the growth of knowledge, because it is the phenomenon of specialisation resulting from the growth of knowledge that makes the repetition and re-presentation necessary.

Conclusions

In this chapter we have attempted to discuss the consequences and implications of the increase of knowledge. We have demonstrated how most, if not all, knowledge grows by a gradual process of cumulation which results in knowledge slowly changing, and have discussed the idea that knowledge may also be subject to sudden revolutionary change. We have also discussed the idea that some knowledge may increase in an additive manner and not be involved in cumulation and consequent change.

The growth of knowledge creates problems for the individual as a consumer of knowledge, one solution to which is increasing specialisation. (Specialisation is therefore a result of, as well as a reason for, the growth of knowledge). Specialisation, however, creates its own problems. The growth of knowledge also affects the structure of social knowledge: not only do individual items of knowledge change, the relationships between individual items of knowledge, and between individual areas of knowledge change; the relationships also become more complex. Growth of knowledge has also produced an increased variety of kinds of documents in which social knowledge is enshrined.

Finally the suggestion was made that specialisation, as a consequence of the growth of knowledge, increases the number of documents necessary to make new knowledge (and knowledge in general) available.

NOTES AND REFERENCES

1 A collection of discussions is given in Sweeney (1966).

2 For further discussion see Kochen (1973), and for an account of an example, see Wyatt (1974). For the 'roots' and 'branches' of an individual's work, see Allison (1967).

3 Weiss (1960). For other discussions see Buckley (1972), Cigánik (1969). Although not specifically on systems, the ideas in Popper (1972) ch 7 are relevant.

4 Blachowicz (1971).

4a See also p 69, and Mitroff (1974).

5 Kochen (1969).

6 Mason (1956) ch 12, 14 and 17 (which are part of a section with the title 'The scientific revolution of the sixteenth and seventeenth centuries'.)

7 Wilson (1973) gives an account; but note also Wesson (1970). Numerous authors, including Ziman (1968) p 56-57 cite this example, which was also the subject of an interesting programme on BBC television.

8 Kuhn (1970, first published 1962). Lakatos (1970) contains discussions of the idea. See also Merton (1973) p 554ff, where Agassi (1971) is described as an 'energetic attack on Kuhn and Lakatos'.

9 Brinton (1950) p 12-17.

10 See however Escarpit (1971), Magee (1973) p 67, and Stent (1972) p 89

10a Watt (1957) p 222 ff.

11 Magee (1973) p 61.

12 Quoted in Shera (1966) p 12.

13 Meier (1961).

14 Ayres (1970)—recommended as light relief.

15 Lindgren (1973) p 318-319; Merton (1973) p 133 and references to Polanyi.

16 Loosjes (1967) p 21.

17 See for example Licklider (1966) and Sparck-Jones (1971).

17a The ideas discussed in this section have a bearing on the notion of 'self-renewing libraries' (*Library Association record*, 78(5) May 1976. 191-194) and underlie criticisms of it. Unless steps are taken to reduce the amount of publication, it would seem impossible to prevent libraries becoming larger. It is possible only to slow down their rate of growth.

18 Harmon (1973): for memory spans, see chapter 5, note 26a.

19 See chapter 5, note 3.

20 Bryan (1968), Green (1964) and Voos (1971).

Chapter 10

THE UNIVERSE OF KNOWLEDGE

INTRODUCTION: In chapter 3, the distinction was drawn between 'personal' knowledge—the knowledge possessed in his mind by an individual, and 'social' knowledge, the knowledge possessed collectively by a society and available to members of a society through its records. We have discussed ideas about the nature and properties of both of these, and made comparisons where appropriate. Generally we have not made any other distinction between possibly different kinds of knowledge, except to describe the philosopher's differentiation between 'private' and 'public' knowledge, and, perhaps more importantly, the distinction which may be made between cumulative and non-cumulative knowledge described in the preceding chapter.

In this chapter we shall examine the assumption that all knowledge—and especially all social knowledge—has the same properties and whether this is justified or not. Are there, in fact, different kinds of social knowledge, or is social knowledge uniform and indistinguishable, except in relation to what it is about? (1) For example, we might say that both of the following statements are about water:

Water is H_2O, a normal oxide of hydrogen.

Water, water, everywhere, nor any drop to drink.

The first of these statements comes from a dictionary of science and the second is a quotation from Coleridge's poem, *The rime of the ancient mariner*. The first question is whether the knowledge contained in these two statements (and more generally the knowledge contained in the documents from which they are taken) is the same kind of knowledge, or does it differ in some *fundamental* respect?

Two other questions follow. Assuming that there are different kinds of knowledge, we have to ask how to distinguish between them? What criteria are there which would enable us to differentiate? What criteria can we use to distinguish the kind of knowledge contained in a dictionary of science, on the one hand, and a book of poetry on the other? The other important question is whether the differences which may exist and the criteria by which they may be distinguished have any relevance to the communication of knowledge. There are some very practical aspects of this question for librarians. For example, very often they arrange and list the documents in their libraries according to classification schemes. Techniques have been devised for drawing up these schemes, and the writer has used them to draw up schemes for bridge-building, marine engineering, motor-vehicle engineering and astronomy (2). These subjects all belong to engineering and science, and may be said to be all the same kind of knowledge (the point is discussed more fully later). The knowledge in Coleridge's poem is not scientific: can the same techniques be applied to the creation of classification schemes for the kind of knowledge contained in that? The same question may be applied to techniques other than classification schemes.

The totality of knowledge is usually referred to, in discussions of these questions, as 'the Universe of Knowledge'. Different kinds of knowledge are referred to as 'disciplines'. The principal advocate of the importance of the matter (in relation to libraries and the knowledge which they contain) is Derek Langridge. In what follows, we shall consider the possibility of the existence of numerous disciplines (and the question thus raised of defining the term 'discipline'); we shall then consider the possibility of the existence of two disciplines, and finally, suggestions that there is, in fact, only one. As usual, our principal concern is with social knowledge, but again it will be necessary to consider the nature of personal knowledge.

Numerous disciplines? the need for a definition

In the introduction, we gave examples of two possibly different kinds of knowledge, or disciplines. It is also necessary to consider the possibility that there may not be just two disciplines, exemplified by the knowledge in a dictionary of science and in a poem, but several, or possibly even a larger number. For example, it may be that the knowledge in the science of astronomy belongs to a different discipline from the knowledge used in building ships, bridges and motor-cars. If it can be said that this particular distinction is possible, then we are likely to be able to say that there are other distinctions which are possible, so that we could conclude that there are numerous disciplines.

In order to discuss this possibility, it is necessary to know what we mean by the term 'discipline' and logically, if we can produce a definition of this term we should find that we have also solved the problem of finding a criterion (or a set of criteria) by which disciplines can be distinguished.

Definitions

At school, pupils study a variety of different subjects: English, history, arithmetic, art, woodwork, chemistry and so on. One use of the term 'discipline' seems to be exactly the same as this use of 'subject', as in the title 'Information science: an emergent discipline'—the only difference is, perhaps, that information science is not the kind of subject normally included in school curricula. In the study of the Universe of Knowledge, however, the idea of disciplines is different from that of subjects in that sense. Physics and chemistry are different school subjects, but in most studies of disciplines they are regarded as belonging to the same discipline, either science or physical science, depending on the viewpoint of the author. For the present purpose, then, 'discipline' is not the same as 'subject'—but what is it?

In the *Oxford English dictionary*, the word 'discipline' in the sense of an area of knowledge is defined as:

a branch of instruction or learning;

a department of learning or knowledge;

a science or art in its educational aspect.

All of these definitions relate to the idea of discipline as the term is used in studies of the Universe of Knowledge. They do not, however, define it in the logical sense of definition (3); they do not indicate the properties possessed by disciplines as a class or set of things, nor do they indicate what distinguishes the knowledge belonging to one discipline from the knowledge belonging to any or all other disciplines. They do not in other words give criteria for differentiating between disciplines.

Another definition sometimes used for discipline is: 'a traditional area of knowledge'. We shall discuss this shortly. The definition which the writer prefers, and which seems to him appropriate in more than one possible sense, is that given by A W Foshay: 'a way of knowing' (23). The implications of this vague phrase, and its relations to social knowledge, will be examined later in some detail.

Nevertheless, our consideration of definitions has not so far produced any criteria sufficient to justify a positive assertion that, for example, the two statements about water, referred to earlier, belong to different disciplines. All we have are some vague phrases which require examination and discussion. We now turn our attention to this and to consideration of other criteria which have been suggested as potential means of distinguishing different disciplines.

141

Traditional areas of knowledge

We have already stated that, so far as the study of the Universe of Knowledge is concerned, disciplines are not the same as subjects in school curricula. If the idea of traditional areas of knowledge is related to the idea of subjects in that sense, then 'traditional areas' is not a satisfactory means of identifying disciplines.

There are, however, a number of other reasons for believing that the traditional areas of knowledge idea is not suitable. The first group of reasons consists of the conclusions reached at the end of the previous chapter—that knowledge changes, that relations between different items of knowledge change, and that the relations tend to become more complex. For an example relating to disciplines, we can consider the subject of psychology, which, as was mentioned in the introduction to chapter 5, was regarded up until the late nineteenth century as a branch of philosophy (which is the reason for its present position on most library shelves). This relationship was changed with the introduction of scientific methods of investigation, and psychology can no longer be regarded as philosophical; it is a science (4). Moreover, it has developed complex relationships with numerous other subjects, not all of which are sciences. Sociology, physiology, linguistics, medicine, anthropology and comparative religious studies are examples which come to mind.

Another source of doubt arises from the consideration of the question 'What tradition'? The writer would himself regard as the three traditional disciplines the areas of science, social science and the humanities; but when reading about American college education, he found a reference to the 'traditional disciplines' of physical, biological and social sciences, and the humanities—four disciplines rather than three. Further, it is difficult to see how there is a continuous (and unchanging) tradition which includes either of these traditions and the 'traditional' trivium and quadrivium of mediaeval education.

A final point is the question of names, and the fact that the same name has been used at different times for studies which are quite different in their content, method and even in their purpose. As an example, Kepler is famous as one of the major contributors to the development of astronomy—but his writings contain such vast quantities of astrological and mystical ideas that if they were published today, astronomers would not wish to have them in their libraries (5). In other words, astronomy and astrology have become entirely separate subjects, although a reference to astronomy in the Middle Ages and even later would have implied the inclusion of astrological ideas. The modern meanings of harmony and harmonics in music and mathematics, and their common ancestry in mediaeval education, are another example of change of this kind.

The idea of disciplines as following and forming a tradition is appealing, but it does not seem to be tenable in the light of even a brief examination.

Degree of certainty

It has been suggested that there is some knowledge about which we can be sure, some about which we can be less sure, and some about which there can be very little certainty indeed. Knowledge may, it is further suggested, be categorised into disciplines according to the amount of sureness or degree of certainty which we attach to it. An inevitable difficulty here would be the decision about the degree of certainty attached to different kinds of knowledge—and the difficulty of reaching any consensus on the matter. How certain can we be, for example, about scientific knowledge, when, as we have seen, its growth depends upon it changing? And how might one persuade the religious believer that his faith depended on anything less than absolute certainty?

'Object known'

Another criterion which has been suggested as a discriminator between disciplines is the 'object known'—what is the knowledge about? A difficulty here is that a problem is raised similar to the one we are trying to resolve: what, in this context, is meant by 'object'? It cannot be the case that only tangible objects are implied, because much of our knowledge is about intangibles—religion, law, music and folklore are all objects of our knowledge. Moreover, in any argument for the existence of numerous different disciplines, we would find that knowledge, in some of the different disciplines proposed, would be about the same tangible objects. Thus in any suggested list of disciplines, poetry and science are regarded as being (or as belonging to) different disciplines, but the quotations from Coleridge's poem (if not the poem itself) and the quotation from the dictionary of science are both about the same object: water.

If, however, this criterion of 'object known' is not limited to tangible objects, then the question is raised of what sorts of objects are appropriate to which disciplines, and, certainly if there are to be numerous disciplines, it does not seem that this does anything more than change the name of the problem. This criterion might, however, be relevant to the case that there are only two disciplines, which is to be discussed later; each of the two is about a different 'object'.

Purpose or aim

Another proposal is that answers to the question 'Why do we want to know?' will be different for different disciplines; and, therefore, the purpose or aim of knowing is a criterion which differentiates disciplines. For example, one reason for wishing to know is the curiosity, mentioned elsewhere, as being a reason for the growth of knowledge—therefore there exists a discipline consisting of knowledge which is learnt and increased for its own sake. Undoubtedly there is a distinction to be drawn between this kind of knowledge, and knowledge which is acquired for practical purposes; between on one hand the knowledge of science, pursued because those concerned desire to know more; and on the other, applied knowledge acquired because it will be useful in making things, or making things better (or in other ways). Thus it is possible to distinguish between 'pure' and 'applied' knowledge, even though the distinction may become blurred, as in chemistry, where knowledge acquired for its own sake is often useful in making new materials available; and knowledge acquired for practical purposes is interesting to those concerned, quite apart from those purposes. It has been claimed that this distinction can be applied to all knowledge. Although there is an application to social sciences (*eg* economic theory and applied economics), it is difficult to imagine applied poetry.

Means of knowing

Another possible criterion to distinguish disciplines is the 'means of knowing'. This is related to the earlier definition of disciplines as 'ways of knowing'; and the meaning is that we can divide the Universe of Knowledge into different disciplines on the basis of answers to questions such as, 'By what means do we know?' 'How do we know?' 'Where does our knowledge come from?' This last question leads to the consideration of 'sources of knowledge' which has already been mentioned (p 36). Different kinds of knowledge might emanate from the various different sources: faith, for example, has already been mentioned as the source of religious knowledge, and reason is the source of knowledge of logical truths; these kinds of knowledge are perhaps to be thought of as different disciplines.

A similar argument was used by Sir Francis Bacon (the same as the philosopher of science mentioned in chapter 6). He, however, used three sources of knowledge: memory, reason, and imagination, and suggested that they gave rise to different kinds of knowledge as follows:

memory —	historical knowledge
reason —	science of philosophy
imagination —	poetry

The further elaborations of Bacon's ideas serve perhaps more to emphasise the earlier point about changes in knowledge and changing relationships between areas of knowledge, rather than to suggest Bacon found a set of disciplines which had a firm and enduring basis. To give just one relevant example, we may note that Bacon gave, as branches of the study of psychology, the study of logic and ethics. These relationships are no longer valid, no matter how sensible they may have appeared in Bacon's time. Nevertheless, we may note that the fundamental tripartite division is regarded as having great and continuing influence.

Nature of the evidence and the method of argument

The foregoing discussion of means of knowing was largely philosophical in its approach, and certainly nothing in it implied that there was justification for the suggestion made earlier that it may be appropriate to define a discipline as 'a way of knowing'. We shall now examine one possible way of expanding that phrase, which produces criteria by which it may be possible to differentiate between disciplines in the Universe of Knowledge.

In chapter 6, scientific knowledge was used as a model or paradigm of all social knowledge. Much of the chapter was devoted to various descriptions of scientific method, which can equally be regarded as the 'source' of scientific knowledge, as 'how' scientists 'know', or as their particular 'way' of knowing. Now, if there are several different disciplines, science is almost certainly one of them (7). (There may be more than one scientific discipline, as mentioned in our earlier discussion of traditional areas of knowledge, but that is a complication which we can ignore for the moment). If science is a discipline, then it may be worth considering 'how scientists know'—their way of knowing—to see what light it might shed on other ways of knowing. How do these other ways, and therefore the disciplines dependent on and derived from them, differ from the way of science and science itself, respectively?

There is no consensus on scientific method; we have ourselves discussed two differing philosophies of science, and there is a vast literature on the subject. Nevertheless scientific *knowledge* depends on:

1 data—collected according to certain rules, which for most practising scientists are unwritten;

2 inferences—drawn according to certain rules which must be seen to be observed.

Popper would not agree—although others might—that this describes the totality of scientific *method*. It ignores the 'problem' and 'criticism' content of World Three, and does not correspond to how science works in practice. Nevertheless science does depend on data, and scientists do, in their reports of their work, draw inferences or conclusions (8).

We suggest that all 'ways of knowing' may be discussed by comparing them with this epitome of the scientific way. In order to make the comparisons easier, the ideas may be expressed in more generally applicable terms:

1 *evidence,* whose collection follows accepted (though not always explicit) standards;

2 *a method of argument* (or discussion) also necessarily subject to certain standards.

Knowledge belongs to a particular discipline according to the nature of the evidence (if any) which it uses, and according to the methods of argument or discussion (if any) which are used in considering the knowledge. These are, it is suggested, criteria which are likely to be of use in distinguishing between a number of different disciplines.

We may demonstrate their applicability by considering four cases of kinds of knowledge which could belong to different disciplines: knowledge of physics, of politics and economics, of history, and of philosophy. The evidence in the case of physics is the results of experiments, which are conducted usually in such a manner as to prevent the results being influenced by extraneous factors (if the experiment is concerned with the effect of temperature, it will be designed to avoid the possibility of pressure affecting the results). In the case of political economics, it is not possible to design or conduct such experiments—it is not possible to set up experimental communist and capitalist states to discover which is the better method of organizing society. Nor can extraneous influences be avoided—the effects of different availabilities of natural resources cannot be precluded from the evidence in the way that the physicist avoids the effect of pressure. Much historical evidence takes the form of documents—and in many instances a difficulty arises because the necessary documents are not available; this affects the method of argument (9). In philosophy, the evidence is often regarded as unimportant—it is only the method of argument which matters.

With regard to the method of argument, we have already discussed elsewhere the methods used in science—the use of induction and deduction. In the case of political economics, the method is affected by the need to make allowances for the effects of extraneous factors: to what extent is the economic success of a government due to the method of government and to what extent is it due to the availability of natural resources (for example)? One of the methods of argument involved in the discussion of historical knowledge is related to missing documents. In the case of such missing evidence the historian may conjecture about what that evidence would be if it were available (by contrast the physicist would attempt to design an experiment in order to discover the necessary evidence). Finally the philosopher, who does not use any evidence (other than examples usually drawn from everyday life), is concerned primarily with the rigour with which other philosophers present their cases.

We suggested that philosophy may be distinguished as a discipline by the fact that in its case no evidence is used. We suggest that in the case of the arts, they are to be distinguished by the fact that they do not use arguments at all. If arts such as music and drama are based on evidence (in a very broad sense), that evidence is the emotions felt by the artist; nor does he attempt to argue about or discuss it, but to create something which will portray those emotions, and, perhaps, will result in the arousal of similar emotions in others. Arts impart emotional knowledge by methods other than argument.

These examples of how we might use the criteria to distinguish different disciplines are not, of course, exhaustive. Even more important, there is no suggestion that the criteria could be used to show that there *are* several different disciplines; even less is it proposed that they enable disciplines to be identified with sufficient precision to allow their number to be counted. It may happen, however, that (even though there is no precise definition) it is necessary to allocate knowledge to different disciplines for practical purposes, as, for example, arranging books on the shelves of libraries (10). In such a circumstance, the criteria of the nature of the evidence and the method of argument, together making up the single criterion of 'way of knowing', and in conjunction with the criterion of purpose or aim, may be useful in deciding how to make this allocation.

The conclusion to be drawn in relation to the first, basic, question asked in the introduction to this chapter, is that the case for the existence of several fundamentally or inherently different disciplines depends on the definition of the term 'discipline', and there seems to be no definition which is generally agreed, or which can be regarded as such in the logical sense of definition.

Two disciplines?

It may be, however, that there are only two disciplines, and it is this possibility which we now consider. We shall discuss numerous suggestions that there are (only) two kinds of knowledge, and the ways in which these are distinguished. The existence of two kinds of knowledge, and their possible relation to the structure of the human brain, has been considered by psychologists and physiologists and we shall examine their hypotheses. We shall also consider some possible consequences of this division. In what follows, we initially ignore the distinction between social and personal knowledge.

Distinctions

There are almost as many suggested means of dividing knowledge into two kinds are there are people who have written on the subject (11). It is not possible to categorise the differences in a comprehensive, thorough-going manner—many of them overlap, and many of them use words whose meaning must be explained by the person who uses them, because they are words which tend to have different implications for different people. The following is intended to convey the general line of thought.

One distinction refers to what the knowledge is about. Some knowledge is about the external world, while some is about the person who knows it. This is the distinction between what philosophers refer to as objective knowledge gained through the senses by the process of perception, and subjective knowledge which is the knowledge of inner consciousness acquired by the process referred to as apperception (see p 38).

Some knowledge is 'intellectual'; other knowledge, by contrast, is 'sensuous' or 'intuitive'. Intellectual knowledge is arrived at by making inferences, by reasoning, as in the case of the sciences, while sensuous knowledge requires the use of imagery and imagination, as in the arts. Inferential knowledge is, as discussed elsewhere (p 124) cumulative, because the newest inferences depend on inferences previously made; on the other hand imaginative knowledge is non-cumulative, because the new 'images' do not depend on the images of the past. Intellectual knowledge is analytic: it tends to proceed on the basis of taking things apart (either physically or figuratively) and seeing how the individual parts work and how they contribute to the things as wholes (compare our discussion of systems, chapter 2). Sensuous, or intuitive knowledge, is holistic; it sees things as indivisible wholes, and does not concern itself with taking them to bits. The drawing of inferences implies a sequence of inferences, so that inferential knowledge may be though of as sequential or linear (note the expression 'lines of thought' in the first paragraph of this section). Imaginative or intuitive knowledge, by contrast, sees things as wholes and, therefore, is able to see them simultaneously.

Some knowledge (and its expression) depends on the use of symbols: *ie* it is verbal or linguistic. Other knowledge cannot or need not be expressed symbolically or verbally: it is non-linguistic, pre-verbal or visual (visual in the sense of pictorial or in the sense of using images as opposed to the use of abstract symbols).

Contrast is often made between 'day' and 'night' or dark and light knowledge; an understanding of the distinction depends, in many of these cases, on a knowledge of the system of philosophy in which they appear. That remark also applies to the difference between Yang and Yin, Yang being a way of knowing which is active, creative and masculine, and connected with Heaven; whereas Yin is a way of knowing which is receptive and feminine, and connected with Earth. Lastly we may note that 'left' and 'right' are often included when ways of contrasting two different kinds of knowledge are being discussed. 'Left' knowledge relates to 'dark' and 'Earth' (note the present English and the original Latin meanings of 'sinister'); 'right' knowledge relates to 'light' and 'Heaven', and generally to things which are good (the meaning of 'dextrous' and the meaning of the Latin word 'dexter' from which it is derived similarly illustrate this point). This is a very ancient distinction, which makes it interesting to note how left and right (without the bad and good implications) reoccur in the more modern ideas discussed in the next section.

Psychology and physiology

The reader may already be familiar with the walnut-like appearance of the brains of higher animals. It should be noted that the brain is like the walnut in consisting of two halves (referred to as hemispheres). Each of the hemispheres controls a different side of the body: the left hemisphere controls the right side of the body, and the right hemisphere controls the left side (12).

Apart from these fairly well known and established notions however, investigations show that the two sides of the brain have different functions (apart from and in addition to the sides of the body which they control); and further, that it is possible for the two hemispheres of the brain to act independently as two separate brains. The evidence for this comes from investigations carried out with patients who have had the tissue which connects the two hemispheres cut, in an attempt to relieve the symptoms either of severe epilepsy or of damage as a result of war wounds or accidents. The result of the operation was not to turn the patients into idiots, but to relieve their symptoms, enabling them to lead more normal lives.

Observations of these patients have been made under controlled conditions when a stimulus was given only to one hand or to one eye (rather than as in normal life to both hands or to both eyes simultaneously).

They appeared to show that the patients reacted to the stimuli as though they had two brains: quite literally, in these cases, the left hand did not know what the right hand was doing; nor did it know what the right eye was seeing, and so on. It also appears that, in adults at least, the ability to use speech is primarily a function of the predominant left hemisphere (the side which controls the right side of the body).

On the basis of evidence like this (and the foregoing was only a very brief summary of part of it) it becomes possible to put forward the hypothesis that there are, in fact, two ways of thinking, and that the two hemispheres are each responsible primarily for one of them. (In fact the evidence further suggests that an individual has two brains which are normally connected and interdependent; but which can act independently, and each of which, moreover, can perform the functions normally performed by the other, should this be necessary as a result of damage caused by disease or injury). It then becomes possible to speculate that the dominant left hemisphere is concerned primarily with activities related to our thinking about and knowledge of, the external world; with our reasoned, intellectual knowledge—the sort which is normally expressed in words or using mathematical symbols. The right hemisphere is concerned with our knowledge of ourselves; of our feelings and emotions, which cannot readily be expressed by language or by language alone, but only in such forms as painting and music.

If further investigations support this dichotomy, it will become apparent that there are different 'ways of knowing' which have a very fundamental basis in human anatomy and physiology; that there are two ways of knowing because, as humans, we have two brains to know with; and because they have differing capacities for knowing different things.

Ways of knowing and 'cultures'

Further consequences follow from this idea, and might even be adduced as evidence for it (13). Western civilization may be readily categorised as being based on science and technology, and concern with the material world which lies outisde the individual human, with the organisation of society and the environment, and with communication between members of societies. In other words, it has been concerned to develop and apply its knowledge of the external world, using rational, inferential methods in the acquisition of that knowledge, and developing and extending the techniques for communicating. The apotheosis of Western culture viewed thus is the famous quotation ' . . . one small step for a man, but one giant leap for mankind'—and the fact that it was possible for millions of people, many thousands of miles away from the speaker, to hear those words almost immediately they were spoken. That achievement depended on the inferentially acquired knowledge of the external world and on a pre-eminence given to organisation and social communication.

Eastern civilisation is not, of course, unconcerned with material things; nor does it lack the ability to organise societies or to communicate. Nevertheless it may be argued that in the East these things are valued much less than they are in Western societies, whose culture can be traced back to the ideas of the philosophers of ancient Greece. In the East, the individual and his knowledge of himself are pre-eminent, and therefore the relevance of the ability to communicate knowledge to others is much less.

The apotheosis of Eastern culture is the holy man in a trance, becoming more and more able to ignore his environment and bodily needs, and therefore more and more able to concentrate on his awareness of himself; and in that state, and subsequently, being unwilling and unable to communicate what he became aware of.

When the differences between Western and Eastern culture are explained and discussed in these terms, it becomes easy to see how they relate to the idea of there being two different ways of knowing, and how it becomes possible for some writers to suggest that Western and Eastern cultures are different because they have given contrasting degrees of importance to the two ways.

Ways of knowing and knowledge

All this has a number of possible bearings on our ideas about social and personal knowledge (in the sense of the distinction we have made between those terms; that of social knowledge being recorded, publicly available knowledge) and on the question of the Universe of Knowledge and its division into disciplines.

Firstly we may ponder on whether social knowledge (by its very nature of being knowledge which people desire, are able, or at least attempt to communicate) is not predominantly knowledge of the rational inferential kind, primarily concerned with the world of things and other people. This argument is in contrast with the point made previously (p 38) where we were at pains to distinguish between our ideas of social knowledge and the philosophical ideas of public objective knowledge. It is necessary, however, before giving an affirmative answer to these questions to remember that Eastern culture does have its own social knowledge in the form of scriptures and philosophical writings, *eg* of the Zen Buddhists. It is also necessary to remember that not all 'documents' are necessarily or primarily verbal—as examples of non-verbal documents one may suggest paintings and musical scores. We should reflect on the increasing availability of such non-verbal media as television; and also remember that such verbal documents as poems and playscripts are often not concerned with objective knowledge, but with the conveying of emotions and impressions, rather than logical arguments about the nature of the external world. We could perhaps then conclude that the existence of social knowledge is likely to be of greater importance in a society interested in the nature of the world in which it exists, than in one in which the most important and most prized knowledge is the knowledge that the individual has of himself.

Secondly, we may suppose that it is possible to argue that the Universe of Knowledge may be divided into two disciplines. One containing rational, external knowledge which is amenable to verbal and symbolic expression, and therefore containing the knowledge of the sciences (which are about the world in which we live) and of the social sciences (which we may categorise by referring to them as being about the mass of other people). The other discipline contains the knowledge of ourselves as individuals, which we gain through our emotions and which artists attempt to portray through music, painting, sculpture, poetry and the like. It might be further suggested that this division, unlike attempts to divide the Universe of Knowledge into a multitude of disciplines, may have as its basis an inherent feature of human mentality—the fact that our brains have two parts, each of which is concerned with knowledge which, when expressed, is regarded as belonging to a different discipline.

Finally, if dichotomy proves unworkable or unsatisfactory, and division into several disciplines appears essential, we might perhaps devise these by referring to a sort of scale having as its extremes entirely rational knowledge of things, and knowledge which is entirely about the individual and which can be conveyed only approximately.

One way of knowing, one discipline?

As well as discussions of the possibility of the existence of different 'ways of knowing' and of different disciplines (and especially of the dichotomy of the Universe of Knowledge into two disciplines, which we will refer to here as science and art) there are also arguments put forward in the literature for the fact that all knowledge has its origins in the same way of thinking; and, therefore, to make clearcut distinctions is erroneous.

The basis of such arguments is that all products of the human intellect, and particularly the great and important ones, depend on imagination and insight (14). Thus our potato plant scientist had insight when he first realised that there could be a connection between the growth of the plant in ashy soil, and the fact that it was growing better than the average plant. Furthermore, this insight was the same kind as that which the playwright uses (or has) when he produces the idea for a play.

In the history and biography of science, there are numerous accounts of the role of insight in the great scientific discoveries; one of the most recent and most discussed is the account of the double-helix arrangement of DNA (the substance which is involved in the transmission of hereditary features) (15). Another famous example is the discovery of the chemical structure known as the benzene ring, in which the atoms in a molecule are connected to each other in a ring. Kekulé, who is credited with this discovery, claimed that the idea came to him in a dream in which he saw a circle of snakes, each with another's tail in its mouth. (Kekulé, as well as being a chemist, had been trained as an architect, which one may imagine gave him an 'eye' for structure and form).

It is also sometimes suggested that the supposed differences between the ways of knowing about sciences and arts is due to the fact that scientists and artists have misleading and inaccurate stereotypes of each other. If they each knew how the other group does work, they might come to realise that the similarities between the methods are greater than the differences. On the other hand, C P Snow is both a novelist and a scientist, and can, therefore, claim to have a foot in both camps. He has written that his experience has convinced him that there are in fact two cultures, an artistic one and a scientific one; and because their ways of knowing and of discussing (and even of behaving) are quite different, there is no common ground between them (15a).

We have already discussed the idea of cumulative and non-cumulative knowledge, and we have noted how the sciences (because they depend on inference) are cumulative; and discussed the suggestion that the arts are non-cumulative. This idea has also been challenged on the basis that the insight of an artist is as dependent on the insights that previous artists have had, as is the insight of a scientist on the insight of previous scientists. It is easy to see that science is cumulative; to find out about DNA it is not necessary to read the original papers on the subject (indeed it would be misleading to use them as a source of current information).

It is not, however, so easy to see how artistic ideas cumulate: nevertheless they do cumulate, inasmuch as, for example, the material for Shakespeare's plays was available in other works of literature (16). Similarly, the writer once went to a film based on the stories of Boccaccio, and at the end remarked (in his innocence) how similar they were in content to Chaucer's *Canterbury tales*, only to have their common ancestry pointed out to him. Artistic works are, therefore, often derivative, not completely original; in a fashion similar to the way in which scientific works are dependent on their predecessors. (The writer would be interested to discover the extent to which the *methods* of artists depend on derivative or even cumulative knowledge—what process was involved in the invention of the novel as an art form?). There is, however, one difference between the sciences and the arts: it is possible to epitomise the meaning of a scientific paper without destroying the meaning of the original. Thus, the statement about benzene rings made earlier includes all the basic information contained in the original paper on the subject. Such epitomes are not possible however for the arts: one cannot reduce the content or meaning of a play by Shakespeare or Shaw to two lines and still convey the impression that the play gives.

One kind of knowledge? indexing and linguistics

In the introduction to this chapter, it was stated that the possibility of the existence of different disciplines—of different kinds or areas of knowledge—was of practical importance to librarians because, if different disciplines exist, it may be necessary to organise the knowledge contained therein in different ways. If, however, it were possible to discover a means of organising knowledge which could cope equally satisfactorily with all knowledge, then it would not be necessary to concern ourselves with the existence of different disciplines or with the means of differentiating between them. In the previous section we examined suggestions that there may be only one discipline; and, here, we shall examine the possibility that a method of indexing may have been found which can deal with all kinds of knowledge because it reflects basic patterns of human communication, that is, the way we think about the things we say.

In the past six years, the PRECIS (Preserved context indexing system) has been developed and applied, in particular to the provision of the alphabetical subject index of the *British national bibliography* (which lists all books published in Britain, except for those issued by central government) (17). Fundamental to the PRECIS system is the use of strings of terms (terms being words which represent parts of the subject being indexed). The order in which the terms appear in a PRECIS string depends on their relationship to the other terms in the 'string'. A pattern of relationships has been devised which covers all the known possible cases, and all the strings must conform to this pattern. Strings (more precisely, secondary strings based on the first) are manipulated by computer to produce index entries (which the computer then sorts alphabetically to produce the index). What concerns us here, however, is the existence of the strings and the pattern which governs the order in which the terms appear in all of them. Further, we can note that this pattern was arrived at pragmatically—that is, it was developed on the basis of practical experience of a number of people over quite a long time (although Austin, who devised the PRECIS system itself, was largely responsible for its final form).

In recent years, the study of linguistics has been considerably influenced by the work of Noam Chomsky, and the idea of transformational grammar (18). An important feature of this work is the suggestion of the existence of 'deep structures'—syntactical forms possessed and used by all members of the human race, and transformed by them, when speaking, into the syntax of the language which they employ. This notion may explain two phenomena: the fact that a child learns the language of his environment, even if this does not happen to be his ancestral language and secondly, the remarkable ability for constructing and understanding utterances that can never have been used before, which is sometimes thought of as a uniquely human ability (though it may not be). These deep structures are envisaged as strings consisting of terms whose relationship with each other determines their position in the string. It is suggested that these strings are innate: they are not learned or acquired by experience, but are one of the mental abilities with which we are born. We may note that, by contrast with the PRECIS strings, the deep structure strings of transformational grammar have been arrived at on theoretical—and perhaps on philosophical—grounds.

The really remarkable observation which results from a comparison of PRECIS and deep structure (DS) strings is that they have the same form, basically (and expressed in terms of English grammar):

object — verb (in passive mood) — subject

for example:

house — (is) built — (by) man

This similarity might of course merely be coincidence: however it is important to realise that PRECIS has been used to produce indexes in a number of different languages and has been found to work in them all. In its use for *British national bibliography*, it has been tested against the entire output of British publishers, which implies a fairly comprehensive coverage of all fields of knowledge. It has also been tested for its capacity to deal with the topics of periodical articles (which often present more difficulties than those encountered in compiling an index to a collection of books), and worked well (which is not to deny that certain changes of detail have been made, but to assert that the basic principle stood up to testing). The same form as in the PRECIS and DS strings can also be seen in the construction of a number of classification schemes and in some indexing methods; all devised before either PRECIS (and its immediate antecedents) or the existence of deep structures had been considered. Further, it has been suggested that when encapsulated information is required, as in press reports and newspaper headlines, the tendency is to use the form of the strings.

None of this is conclusive evidence; but it does contain the makings of at least a hypothesis that in the PRECIS system 1) we have an information-processing system (a system for handling knowledge) which replicates an innate human information-processing system; 2) we have a system which is universal: it can be applied to all languages and all subjects; and 3) in relation to the present context, we have a system which works without taking account of the existence of disciplines or of the differences between them and the knowledge which they contain. (We must remember, however, that in our discussion of the possible existence of two disciplines or cultures, the suggestion was made that some knowledge is non-verbal and non-linguistic: whether this makes any differences to these hypothetical claims for the PRECIS system is a matter to be considered) (23).

Sociological approach

To a very considerable extent, the assumption of the foregoing discussion is that personal knowledge and social knowledge are similar, if not identical, in the question of the existence of disciplines; and in view of the relationship between them, this may be a reasonable assumption. A further assumption, implicit in much if not all of the discussion, is that we find out first about personal knowledge, and then proceed to discuss social knowledge.

It may be, however, that this is the wrong way round, and that the existence of disciplines in knowledge should be examined by firstly investigating social knowledge. The sociology of knowledge already has a considerable literature (20) and there are investigations of the sociology of science and social science, and such matters as the different uses made of literature by both scientists and engineers. All of this tends to proceed from the assumption of the existence of different disciplines; scientists and social scientists are identified *first*, and then compared (21). It might be worthwhile to turn these investigations around, examine various social factors (communication patterns being obviously especially relevant) and *then* try to identify discipline groups on the basis of the results.

Conclusions and summary

In this chapter we have discussed the need for and the possibility of, dividing the Universe of Knowledge into a number of different disciplines (or areas or kinds of knowledge). Very little has been said about the number of disciplines which there might be, but cases can be made out, on the basis of the evidence available, either for the existence of several disciplines (but not perhaps for the existence of a large number), or of two only. A case can also be argued for there being no disciplines; or for it not being necessary to concern ourselves with their existence, because it is possible to devise a system for handling knowledge without taking their existence into consideration.

If there are several disciplines, it is necessary firstly to define what is meant by 'discipline'—there is no ready-made dictionary definition which represents a consensus of what is meant when the term is used in the context of discussions of the Universe of Knowledge. Of numerous suggestions for criteria by which the knowledge belonging to different disciplines may be differentiated, the most likely candidate appears to be the idea of 'way of knowing'. This phrase implies the use or non-use of evidence and argument, according to rules, in ways which differ for each discipline. If there are numerous disciplines, they, and the relationships between them, are liable to change with time.

There may, however, be only two disciplines—or two 'ways of knowing' (the phrase seems particularly suggestive in this context). This might well be a reflection of the fact that there are basically two human thought processes, which itself may be a reflection of the way in which the human brain is structured. These two ways of knowing may have resulted in the development of different human cultures. Again, however, it may be that, for practical purposes, (and for reasons which are fundamental to human nature), it is not necessary to distinguish different disciplines. None of these conclusions may be regarded as final; most of them, indeed, can only be regarded at the moment as tentative and a further tentative suggestion for a new approach to the problem has been given.

Social knowledge: division by use

Quite apart from the division of the Universe of Knowledge into disciplines, there exists the possibility of the division of personal and social knowledge into categories according to the use made of them. Personal knowledge may be divided into categories such as personal (the dates of family birthdays), work (in the writer's case, familiarity with cataloguing rules) and recreational (knowledge of the rules of Association Football).

Similar categories can be devised for social knowledge, and have applications when we discuss its communication (22). The four categories of use suggested are:

Research;

Education (formal education);

Culture (informal education);

Entertainment.

Research workers or scholars use the social knowledge available to them as a source of information and ideas to be used to further their own work, which is basically the creation of new knowledge. This knowledge is new, not only to the individual research worker, but also to society, and may be referred to as 'socially new knowledge'. Students following formal courses of education also use social knowledge as a source of ideas, but in this case the knowledge acquired is not socially new, but new only to the individual learner. This use of social knowledge involves its dissemination to an enlarged audience, rather than the creation of completely new social knowledge.

Culture is a term which has a number of different meanings, but the idea which we try to convey by its use here is the idea of self-education, of self-improvement, of education not in connection with any formal course of instruction. Entertainment on the other hand means simply what its name implies—the use of knowledge (in the broadest sense of the term) for amusement and recreation.

Although it is possible, and may sometimes be useful, to make these distinctions, it is clear that there cannot be any hard and fast lines drawn between them. The same user may use the social knowledge contained in a library for different purposes *eg* when he visits it to find some piece of information *and* takes the opportunity to borrow a book on chess. The use of knowledge made by the research student falls between the categories of education and research, as he is concerned both with increasing his own knowledge and with the creation of socially new knowledge.

The same document may be used for all four categories of purpose. The scholar may borrow an edition of Marlowe's plays to further his study of the language of Elizabethan England. A student may use them because they are a set text. Another person may read them because he wants to extend his cultural awareness, while another may do so simply because he enjoys it (not, of course, that the acquisition of 'culture' is necessarily unenjoyable). However, in different libraries and in different situations, different uses may predominate.

NOTES AND REFERENCES

1 Langridge (1969). Richardson (1930) is a classical historical bibliography of classification schemes. Ziman (1968) ch 2 is relevant, because he relates other kinds of knowledge than scientific to his idea of consensus. Bormann (1965) ch 3, Hirst (1974) esp ch 6 and Pantin (1968) are examples of the numerous other discussions.

2 Vickery (1961) discusses the technique applied to the subjects.

3 Stebbing (1966) ch 6.

4 Murphy (1972) especially ch 11—Wundt and the rise of experimental psychology.

5 Mason (1956) p 106-107.

6 Compare Maltby (1975) p 55.

7 Ziman (1968) ch 2 and p 74ff.

8 Popper (1972) p 186.

9 For discussions of 'evidence' and 'method of argument' in relation to history, see Hays (p 181-227) and Thernstrom (p 59-76), both in Lipset (1968).

10 Maltby (1975) p 294 and *passim* emphasises the importance of disciplines in relation to library classification; see also Bliss (1929) p 205-211. The idea is also of importance in communication practice and studies of information exchange, *eg* Garvey (1970) and Jones (1972).

11 Ornstein (1972) p 67 and *passim*. For readings see Ornstein (1973). See also Bruner (1962) whose title is significant.

12 Gazzaniga (1967), Bogen (1969). Both appear in Ornstein (1973) p 87-100 and 101-125 respectively. See also Eccles (1965) and Hebb (1972) p 49-53.

13 Ornstein (1973) p 65 and 214-215. See also the account by Lee (1950), reprinted as ch 10 in the same book, and in Carpenter (1970) p 136-154, where it is followed by comments by Robert Graves.

14 Koestler (1966); Guilford (1968); and Stent (1972), especially p 89.

15 Olby (1974), Watson (1968).

15a Snow (1964).

16 See chapter 9, note 10.

17   Austin (1975).   For a bibliography, see Larsen (1976).

18   Chomsky (1971); Lyons (1970); Greene (1972).   Gregory (1974) p 624ff discusses the hypothesis that the deep structure evolved from perception mechanisms; this may be viewed as strengthening the argument.   For general reviews of linguistics in relation to information science, see Montgomery (1972) and Foskett (1970). Hutchins (1975); Fishman (197?

19   The ideas are discussed by Austin in his paper *Citation order and linguistic structure* which will appear in the forthcoming *Festschrift for John Metcalf* (editor W B Rayward) to be published by the Australian Library Association.

20   Merton (1973).

21   *Eg* Skelton (1973).

22   Saunders (1971).

23   Foshay (1962).

Chapter 11

REVIEW, COMMENTS AND CONCLUSIONS

INTRODUCTION: In this final chapter we draw together various threads
to produce a survey of the nature and properties of knowledge in general,
and of social knowledge in particular. Some of these may seem obvious
and commonsense, but as was indicated in the introduction and discussed
on p 93 ff, commonsense, obvious arguments still deserve examination.
They are sometimes wrong, and when they do survive scrutiny they can,
as a result, be expressed with greater conviction. One of the conclusions,
however, runs contrary to an idea of one of the most influential writers
on the organisation of knowledge, H E Bliss, and another explains why
this might be so.

The ideas which we present here were first put into their present form
some years ago, and are put forward in the knowledge that only a small
fraction of the vast amount of relevant literature has been examined.
Nevertheless, they seem to represent a consensus—they do appear elsewhere in the literature, even if it is rare to find them drawn together in
the way that we are attempting (1).

What is knowledge?
The first conclusion arrived at, with some certainty, is that it is difficult
and probably impossible to find a definition of knowledge which would
be universally accepted by all philosophers. Such a lack of agreement
among philosophers does not, however, preclude the investigation and
discussion of the nature and properties of knowledge by means other than
those of philosophers. For the purposes of such discussion it is suggested
that knowledge be considered as, firstly, what a person believes and states
as his belief (or what people collectively believe and state). Secondly,
and in accordance with Popper, that the extent to which statements are
to be regarded as knowledge depends on the extent to which those statements are true; the judgement of the truth of a statement being based on
the extent to which it is compatible with other statements that are believed

to be true. It must be emphasised that this is not propounded as an exact definition which is logically indisputable, but merely as a kind of working model, in connection with which various properties can be discussed.

Social and personal knowledge

For the practical purposes of those who are concerned with the communication of knowledge, which includes librarians and information scientists, it seems at least useful and probably essential, to distinguish between two different kinds of knowledge, whose nature and properties are in many ways analogous, but are in one way distinct: personal knowledge and social knowledge.

Personal knowledge exists in the minds of individuals and is, at least in the first instance, available only to the person who knows it. Social knowledge is the knowledge possessed collectively by a society, and is available freely and equally to all members of that society through its records. The knowledge which I have in my mind is my personal knowledge: the knowledge in the documents in a library (which are freely and equally available records of the society formed by the users and potential users of the library) is part of the social knowledge of that society.

The two kinds of knowledge are neither mutually exclusive nor independent. Much of the knowledge I have in my mind is social knowledge in the sense that it can be found in documents; most of the knowledge which exists in the world's libraries is also known in or by the mind of some person, somewhere, and so is also personal knowledge. Social knowledge depends for its existence on personal knowledge; much personal knowledge is derived from social knowledge. By making a record of some of my personal knowledge, I can turn it into social knowledge, but this personal knowledge was gleaned (in part at least) from the records of the society to which I belong. These distinctions and relationships are made in a dichotomous, black-and-white sort of way: on close examination there is a grey area between the extremes. Also, as discussed later, it is possible to take more than one view of social knowledge.

Knowledge and organisation

Organisation is an essential property of knowledge. If its individual constituents are not organised into a coherent whole, then no knowledge exists. We have seen that this idea appears in the psychology of learning. The details of the process may not be clearly understood, but there is little doubt that the formation of concepts depends on the organisation of percepts: the abstraction/discrimination and generalisation/grouping process that has been discussed is an organisational process. The same idea is expressed differently when we refer to the drawing of inferences. Inferring implies the making of a relationship between two things; for example, between the soil in which a plant grows and the size or speed of the growth of the plant. Although we discussed the drawing of inferences in the context of scientific knowledge, it is not a process which occurs only in that context, but is a normal daily activity in adults, as well as an ability whose development can be observed in children. Our bus traveller Mr Bloggs developed and used it in connection with his expeditions.

Organisation is implicit in Popper's discussion of the nature of truth: if statements are true to the extent to which they are compatible with other statements which are believed to be true, then it is necessary to relate, or organise, statements so that they can be shown to support and depend on each other. The idea is made explicit in Ziman's account of science as Public Knowledge: 'the citation of references embeds [a scientific paper] in the pre-existing consensus. The orderliness of this process, the intellectual structure in the library, the catalogue, the index, the encyclopaedia, the treatise, give meaning to the research of the past ... The mere accumulation of miscellaneous details is not enough to provide such order and meaning.' We can say simply: no organisation, no knowledge.

Knowledge as a system

That knowledge is a coherent whole, formed by the organisation of its individual constituents, implies that knowledge can be regarded as a system; because such a structure is the first part of the definition of a system. The idea has also been discussed in the literature (see also p 124, 135). The consequence of being able to view knowledge as a system is that we may expect it to have at least some of the properties of systems. In particular, the growth of knowledge and the implications of that growth are ideas which are given additional credence by the ability to take this view. In turn (and we can note this as an example of the idea of knowledge as mutually supporting and dependent statements) the evidence that knowledge grows and becomes more complex in the process confirms that we are correct in supposing that it forms a system.

Knowledge is not absolute

There is a great deal of evidence to suggest that knowledge is not absolute, that it is different at different times and in different environments.

The idea of change is implicit in the ability to learn: we have
referred to the fact that, in adults especially, learning involves changing
existing concepts (or knowledge) rather than the acquisition of completely new concepts. An adult who learns that a dolphin is a mammal,
more like himself than the fishes the dolphin superficially resembles, and
whose surroundings the dolphin shares, is involved with changing his
existing concept or knowledge. We can also say that when the same
fact became part of the consensus, a change was made in social knowledge.

In addition, however, change is not just a question of change of
individual items of knowledge; it is also, or it implies or involves, changes
in the relationships between individual items. At the level of personal
knowledge, our discussion of concepts shows that the learning about
dolphins example involves changing relationships between concepts.
Some mental process of deleting the relationship 'dolphin-is-a-kind-of-
fish' and changing it to 'dolphin-is-a-kind-of-mammal' takes place.
Such changes in relationships also occur in social knowledge, and
affect not only comparatively small areas of knowledge such as what
sort of creatures dolphins are, but also the relationships between whole
fields of human study and endeavour; such as the example of philosophy-
psychology and science-psychology which we used earlier in discussing
the idea of disciplines as traditional areas of knowledge (other examples
were given there).

This idea runs contrary to the notion propounded by H E Bliss, and
referred to by him as the stability of the educational and scientific
consensus, that changes in the relationships between areas of knowledge
were unlikely (3). The writer has considerable admiration for the works
of Bliss (and for the devotion he must have given to their production)
but in this particular instance he seems to have been wrong. Curiously
though, his error in this is perhaps itself an example of the fact that
knowledge changes. There was a time, in the 1890s and a while after,
when it was generally regarded as true that the educational and scientific consensus was stable; that any new knowledge would fall into the
pattern of the existing knowledge and would not affect the relationships established in that pattern (4). It is reasonable to surmise that it
was in this period that Bliss formulated his ideas, even though his major
works did not appear until almost the 1930s, by which time the consensus had at least begun to change.

Knowledge depends on environment

Knowledge is also not absolute, in the sense that it differs in different places and environments and in different societies, as we tried to show in the discussion of how social factors affect knowledge. The social knowledge of North America is different from the social knowledge of Europe; the social knowledge of France is different from the social know-. ledge of Great Britain; the social knowledge of economists is different from the social knowledge of astronomers, regardless of where they live, and so on. This, of course, affects the personal knowledge of individual North Americans, Europeans, Frenchmen, Britons, economists and astronomers; and the personal knowledge of a French economist will be more different from the personal knowledge of an American astronomer than from the personal knowledge of a French astronomer.

Such differences do not only affect knowledge in relation to social systems such as are constituted by countries and groups of scholars, they also affect the knowledge within smaller groups, who may be regarded as subsystems. Thus, even within the same community, the knowledge of different groups within it, and of the individual members of the groups, may be affected. These groups may be distinguished by such things as class, colour and creed. As an example, we may refer to different attitudes to (or knowledges about) the police among different sections of the community. The extent to which differences between groups is of importance to librarians might be argued. It is relevant to note however that there have been criticisms of the Dewey Decimal Classification (which is used to arrange the stock of virtually every British public library) not only on the grounds of bias towards the USA, but also on the grounds of bias towards white, Anglo-Saxon and Protestant cultural groups.

Knowledge as what is socially accepted

If we accept that knowledge changes with time and environment, then we may further conclude that knowledge consists of what is socially accepted as such. The idea of social acceptance is also implicit in our working definition of knowledge given at the beginning of the chapter.

Thus the knowledge of the Trobriand Islanders in 1900 was knowledge because it was believed or accepted as such by them at that time. That it is so different from the knowledge of our forefathers in 1900, or from that of the Trobriand Islanders now, does not affect the matter. This

165

particular example is not very relevant to social knowledge as recorded knowledge, but the remark is also true of such a relevant example as the knowledge which would have been available in an Oxford College, and on the shelves of its library, in 1500.

The idea of social acceptance is not, however, to be found only in writings of social anthropologists and social psychologists; it is also implicit in the Popperian definition of truth. If knowledge consists of what is true, and if truth consists of statements which are compatible with other statements which are believed to be true, then knowledge depends for its existence on the social acceptance of the compatibility of statements. In practice, it is not the case that statements are compatible simply because J Bloggs says that they are compatible; rather they are accepted because the majority of those who are able to judge their compatibility agree with him. The same argument underlies Ziman's concept of Public Knowledge as a consensus. The best example of the idea of the social acceptability of social knowledge is the set of statements drawn together in a unity by an expert into an advanced monograph which is regularly consulted and cited by other experts. This stirs in the author's memory a recollection of a scientist of some considerable standing saying to a young post-graduate student, and referring to a very famous book in their field, 'look it up in Chandrasekhar: if it's in there, it's probably correct'.

In some cases, the society at large may be able to judge the acceptability of statements. In cases where the statements refer to matters regarded as being the concern of experts, then social acceptance also involves the willingness of the non-experts to accept the judgements of the experts (and, therefore, their belief in the experts' expertise).

Growth, cumulation and change

Regardless of the basis used for the measurement of the quantity of available knowledge, the evidence indicates that the quantity has continually increased in the past and that the increase has been exponential rather than linear. In the case of one of the indices used—the numbers of documents—it has been suggested that it exaggerates the rate of growth of knowledge; but, while the argument may have some foundation, we have tried to show that at least some of the 'unnecessary' duplication of publication of knowledge is itself symptomatic of the growth of knowledge and the resulting specialisation of interests.

The enlargement of knowledge does not consist merely, to re-quote Ziman, of the accumulation of miscellaneous facts; it is a process of cumulation, of growth in the sense in which that word is applied to living organisms. New knowledge depends on existing knowledge and is assimilated into it; thereby expanding it and, frequently, modifying it. The cumulative effect of such modifications is that, however slight they may individually have been, collectively they will eventually be sufficient to change the previously existing knowledge completely. The process was exemplified by the discussion of the case of van Maanen: what was true in 1910 was gradually eroded away by new items of knowledge, so that by about 1930 it was completely untrue; that is, it was no longer regarded as knowledge.

The idea of growth, cumulation and change is certainly to be seen in the fields of scientific and technical knowledge. It is less obvious in the case of the humanities, and indeed it has been claimed that knowledge can be divided into two kinds: cumulative, as in science, and non-cumulative, as in the arts. Examples can be found to support this view. Contrarily, it is possible to suggest that the content of the knowledge contained in the arts is to some extent cumulative: literary critics who refer to the influence of one writer on another supply some of it.

Different kinds of knowledge

The previous remarks lead into the discussion of the existence of different kinds of knowledge: is it possible, and for practical purposes is it necessary, to make any differentiation of knowledge into different types, other than the differentiation into personal knowledge and social knowledge?

It seems that there is no agreement on the answer to this question, nor is there any agreement on how we may define the term 'discipline', used to refer to the different kinds of knowledge. It was suggested that perhaps the best definition is 'way of knowing', and that this might be interpreted as referring to the kinds of evidence used in different disciplines, and to the method of argument—the rules imposed by the discipline on the discussion of that evidence. To this might be added the idea of the purpose or aim of acquiring the knowledge.

Three different possibilities were examined with regard to the actual existence of disciplines: firstly that there are several, secondly that there are two, and thirdly that, at least for the purpose of organising knowledge, there are none and that all knowledge can be regarded as homogeneous. We have not been able to find or make any convincing argument to support the view that there are numerous *essentially* different disciplines, although the definition of disciplines that has been given might be a convenient method of distinguishing between different kinds of knowledge, if it were necessary to do so.

Reasons for supposing that there are two kinds of knowledge are partly philosophical, but there is at least some evidence from psychology and physiology that in the structure of the human brain there exists the potential for being two kinds of (personal) knowledge, which might give rise to two different kinds of social knowledge. Possible social consequences of this were discussed. The reason for regarding knowledge as homogeneous rests largely on the similarity between certain features of a recently developed method of indexing and of a hypothesis put forward by an eminent linguist as an explanation of the human capacity to learn and use language. For both of these arguments it is necessary to make the point that the evidence is sufficient to justify further investigation, but not enough for firm conclusions to be drawn. The possibility of investigating the idea of disciplines by sociological methods was mooted.

There is, however, one important distinction—that between data and inferences—which applies not only to science, but to any area of knowledge using measurement. Data are the raw material of knowledge; it is the inferences based on them which constitute knowledge. Nevertheless the data must be available. In practical terms, we should note that it is sometimes necessary to distinguish between two different kinds of 'information systems': data retrieval systems, which can produce answers to such questions as how many fourteen year-old girls in London wear spectacles; and reference retrieval systems, which supply, in response to questions, details of documents (and occasionally the documents themselves) in which a particular item of knowledge can be found.

Another, quite different, approach is to distinguish between the uses made of social knowledge: research (which produces more knowledge); educational (in the formal sense); cultural (in the sense of informal education) and for entertainment. In relation to the latter, we may note that even the most 'light' light reading (or viewing) may form part of social knowledge, because it can be regarded as part of 'the entire cultural heritage'. The extent of the truth of this can be realised when it is remembered that the nineteenth century equivalents of the *Dandy* and the *Beano* are now used as sources of social history.

The function of libraries
Although the matter is outside the scope of this book, a study of communication shows that the function of libraries is to facilitate the communication of social knowledge for the uses just described. (It can

also be shown they facilitate communication over time, from one generation to the next, and that they enable the individual to have access to much more knowledge than would be possible if they did not exist) (4a). To this end they carry out four operations:

acquisition
preservation
organisation
dissemination

Acquisition is the process of actually obtaining the documents or social knowledge. Preservation means ensuring the documents and the knowledge which they contain continue to exist. Organisation means generally the physical arrangement of the documents and the making of lists of them and of the ideas or knowledge which they contain, so that the documents themselves and the knowledge can be found. The operation of dissemination involves informing users and potential users of the documents and the knowledge, and the promotion of their use.

Selection is a subsidiary process in all four operations. Libraries select the documents which they are to acquire; select the documents which they will preserve; organise some documents more carefully than others; and choose which documents or ideas are disseminated to whom.

Finally, we may note the distinction between data and knowledge; the two are not the same, and neither are the techniques for handling them. In particular, present technology enables us to cope with data more easily than with social knowledge; and, for various reasons, this technology has been developed and operates largely independently of libraries. Whether this is to be applauded or deplored is a matter of debate, but it is something which cannot be ignored by librarians.

Libraries and the properties of social knowledge

Our conclusions may be seen as confirming two prejudices in the librarian. Firstly, we have found (unsolicited) support for the belief that knowledge matters; and that social knowledge, as distinct from personal knowledge, matters: it has the advantages of being more enduring and being more widely available.

Secondly, organisation is a basic operation within libraries, and we have seen that this is an essential property of knowledge. We are not, in performing this task in libraries, doing something unnatural or imposing some artificial restraint on knowledge; we are, rather, creating or maintaining it, or helping to do so.

169

Social knowledge may be seen as documents containing knowledge which, at the time, is believed to be credible: that is, it corresponds to Ziman's Public Knowledge as being the current consensus. Alternatively, it may be seen as including any document which forms part of the 'entire cultural heritage': which is to say, it corresponds to Popper's World Three. A library pursuing a policy based on the first, Public Knowledge, image will discard documents and may be highly selective in carrying out its operations. One based on the alternative World Three view will attempt to be comprehensive (to collect rather than to select in relation to acquisitions) and will be especially concerned with preservation.

Growth

In *either* case, the growth of social knowledge has three effects. Firstly, there is the straightforward problem of storage—where to put it all. Secondly, selection becomes both more imperative and more difficult: inevitably individual libraries process a smaller proportion of a larger mass of knowledge. Thirdly, for these reasons there is a tendency to co-operation or integration on a local, regional, national and international basis with individual libraries ceasing to regard themselves as entirely separate systems, and adopting the view that they are parts of larger systems (or networks). This may take the form of sharing responsibilities or of the creation of centralised agencies. Many recent developments in librarianship may be seen in this light (4b).

The question of the existence of disciplines seems to be a matter for further investigation, whose results the librarian must await.

Change and the organisation of knowledge

An important implication is that the organisation of knowledge must change. Social knowledge changes and not only changes in detail, such as would require only minor changes in the way in which it is organised in libraries, but often major alterations to the relationships between different fields of learning; as when two areas of knowledge, previously seen as distinct, fuse together to form a new area. Moreover, change is a consequence of growth; and the growth of knowledge is exponential, so that the rate of change becomes more and more rapid. We might surmise that the amount of change which has taken place in the past thirty years is as great as the change which occurred in the preceding hundred years, and that it will be equalled by the amount which takes place in the next ten. As a consequence, methods devised for organising knowledge at the beginning of a librarian's career, and then considered as good as possible, are likely to need to be changed several times before his retirement.

The further implication of this is that systems for organising knowledge should either be regarded as disposable, or else they should incorporate the maximum number of features necessary to allow them to be changed with the minimum of effort and expense. For example, the devising and implementation of any new general classification should be carried out in such a way that frequent and wholesale revision should be possible, and economically feasible, for every new edition. It is already possible to see how this could be achieved. We should note, incidentally, that there is a reverse side to this coin: methods of organisation devised for the current consensus will not necessarily be suitable for documents published fifty or even twenty years before: the author can vouch for that from personal experience of revising classification schemes.

The effect of environment

Another implication is that because knowledge is different in different environments—in the case of libraries, for the different communities served—its organisation may need to be different in those different environments. This is the same idea as that put forward by Bliss as the principle of 'relative classification'; and is related to the idea of Cutter's Expansive Classification (5). Exactly to what extent it is necessary to put this principle into practice, and to what extent it is economically justifiable to do so, is not clear and may need investigation; but methods for use in Harvard University Library are not likely to be the most effective methods for Little Piddlecombe branch of Bumbleshire County Libraries, or for the library of the Research Department of Shoe Pharmaceuticals Ltd. At the present time, the adoption of computer methods in libraries is tending towards the standardisation of practice. The time may come, however, when this is reversed, and the ability of a computer to vary its output is much more used that it is at present in this connection.

How effective can information systems be?

The effectiveness of information (retrieval) systems, referred to earlier as 'reference retrieval systems', seems generally to run in the sixty to eighty percent range; for example, of every five appropriate documents, the system finds details of three or four (6). It has been a matter of concern that it has not been possible to find a system which is one hundred percent effective, and retrieves all five documents. However, it may be that our systems are not so bad after all, because the same level of efficiency seems to obtain for the human brain, which is usually considered to be the best known mechanism for handling information (7).

This may suggest that it is futile to attempt to devise more effective systems; because, no matter to what extent such systems are 'automated', they all involve, and always must involve, a fundamental proportion of human effort. If the system is intended to *operate* with the minimum of human effort (and interference), then the effort involved in its *initial design and implementation* will increase. For example, if a system is to retrieve documents concerned with sheep, then to achieve one hundred percent effectiveness the term 'sheep' must somewhere and somehow and sometime be linked in the system with the term 'ram'. This linkage must be made during the operation of the system by the users or operators, or it must be built in by its designers; in either case, the linkage is one which must be made by a human mind. (In the systems which are based on automatic examination of the texts of documents, the human minds involved are those of the authors of the documents and of the designers of the systems.)

Connotation/denotation: relevance/pertinence

In discussing concepts, we drew attention to the notions of denotation and connotation. The relations between these terms, and further relationships between them and other pairs of terms, and their significance for and in libraries have been discussed elsewhere (8). Essentially we may say that denotation is connected with the idea of 'relevance': the fact of whether a particular document is appropriate to the *stated request* of a user; while the idea of connotation is connected with the idea of 'pertinence': the fact of whether the document is appropriate to the *actual needs* of the user, which needs may be, for one reason or another, unexpressed or unexpressable. The difference between relevance and pertinence is, we suggest, of significance both for research into, and the actual practice of, librarianship.

More and more difficult

The final implication is rather gloomy. One of the consequences of the growth of knowledge is that social knowledge becomes more and more complex. The problems of organising knowledge are, therefore, not only those of handling increased quantity, but of dealing with a more complex structure. A doubling in size of the quantity of knowledge will not merely double the difficulty of organising it, it will quadruple it; and a tripling in quantity will involve a ninefold increase in the problem of organisation.

Envoi

These conclusions are only part of the intended message. The other equally important part is that knowledge of knowledge, whose importance was discussed in the introduction, cannot be acquired by librarians by studying only the literature of librarianship, or for that matter by adding to it a study of philosophy. Consideration of the properties of knowledge (and of how it is communicated) is the concern of many occupations other than that of librarian—of psychologists, sociologists, of linguistics scholars and communication engineers and many others. The knowledge which they have amassed as a result of their investigations forms a vast reservoir of ideas which librarians and information scientists may use to formulate their understanding of what their function is, and how best to perform it.

In this book we have concerned ourselves almost entirely with the broad issues of the nature of knowledge, but other branches of learning can also help with comparative details of technique. An outstanding example is that for nearly seventy years librarians have been trained to believe that the notations of classification schemes should be 'simple and brief'; but only rarely has any attempt been made to define simplicity and brevity or to say how simple and brief notations should be. However, there now exists a considerable amount of relevant knowledge, based on objective experiments (as opposed to subjective opinions) available in the literature of psychology (9). More generally, librarians devote considerable time and effort to learning about, improving and developing techniques of classification; but their efforts have taken very limited account of the work of others concerned with classification, such as biological taxonomists and psychologists investigating the role of classification in human information processing.

A century ago it may well have been the case that other fields of scholarship could not tell librarians anything which could enable them to improve the effectiveness of their services; but knowledge grows and changes, and it ought not be supposed that we need still rely entirely on our own efforts. The infant information science or 'informatics' will at best grow up very slowly, and may even suffer premature death, unless it takes in nourishment from as many and as various foster-parents as possible.

NOTES AND REFERENCES

1 Sampson (1971) p 29-222.
2 Ziman (1968) p 103-104.
3 Bliss (1939) p 42.

4 Jordan (1911).

4a Saunders (1972).

4b Gray (1975) ch 4.

5 Bliss (1939) p 43.

6 Cleverdon (1970), Vickery (1970).

7 Lindsay (1972) p 349ff (and also p 428-433).

8 Kemp (1974); see also Lesk (1969).

9 See chapter 5, note 27.

BIBLIOGRAPHY

(Place of publication is London, unless otherwise stated)

ADAMS, R M 'The origin of cities' *Scientific American* 203 (3) September 1960. 153-168.

AGASSI, J 'Tristam Shandy, Pierre Menard and all that: comment on *Criticism and the growth of knowledge*' *Inquiry* 14 1971. 152-164.

AITCHISON, J *General linguistics* (Teach Yourself Books, 1972).

ALLISON, D 'The growth of ideas' *International science and technology* July 1967. 24-32 (especially diagram p 25).

AMERICAN SOCIETY FOR INFORMATION SCIENCE *Key papers in information science,* editor Arthur W Elias (New York, American Society for Information Science, 1971).

ANGRIST, S W and HEPLER, L G *Order and chaos: laws of energy and entropy* (Penguin, 1973).

ANTHONY, L J 'Purpose in cooperation' *Aslib proceedings* 21 (11) November 1969. 454-463.

ANTHONY, L J *et al* 'Growth in the literature of physics' *Reports on progress in physics* 32 (6) December 1969. 709-767.

ASHEIM, L *The humanities and the library: problems in the interpretation, evaluation and use of library materials* (Chicago, ALA, 1957).

ASHER, E J *Introduction to general psychology* (Boston, Heath, 1953).

ASHWORTH, W 'The information explosion' *Library Association record* 76 (4) April 1974. 63-68, 71.

AUSTIN, D *PRECIS: a manual of concept analysis and subject indexing* (British Library, Bibliographic Services Division, 1974).

AYER, A J *The problem of knowledge* (Penguin, 1956).

AYRES, F H 'Some basic laws of library automation' *Program* 4 (2) April 1970. 68-9.

BARBER, B and HIRSCH, W *The sociology of science* (NY, Free Press of Glencoe, 1962).

BARRY, G *et al,* editors *Communication and language* (Macdonald, 1965).

175

BASSEY, M *Science and society* (University of London Press, 1968).

BEARD, R M *An outline of Piaget's developmental psychology* (Routledge and Kegan Paul, 1969).

BEAUJEU-GARNIER, J *Geography of population* (Longmans, 1966).

BEISHON, J *Systems* (Bletchley, Open University Press, 1971) (Open University Technology Foundation Course, Unit 1; T 100 1).

BEISHON, J and PETERS, G, editors *Systems behaviour* (Harper & Row, for Open University Press, 1972).

BELL, D *The reforming of general education* (Columbia University Press, 1966).

BERGEN, D 'Implications of general system theory for librarianship and higher education' *College and research libraries* 27 (5) 1966. 358-388.

BERGEN, D 'The communication system of the social sciences' *College and research libraries* 28 (4) July 1967. 239-252.

BERTALANFFY, L von *General system theory: foundations, development, applications* (Allen Lane/Penguin Press, 1971; NY, Brazilier, 1968).

BLACHOWICZ, J A 'Systems theory and evolutionary models of the development of science' *Philosophy of science* 38 (2) June 1971. 178-199.

BLISS, H E *Organization of knowledge and the system of the sciences* (NY, Holt, 1929).

BLISS, H E *The organization of knowledge in libraries* 2nd edition (NY, Wilson, 1939).

BOGEN, J E 'The other side of the brain: an appositional mind' *Bulletin of the Los Angeles Neurological Society* 34 (3) July 1969. 135-162 (also in Ornstein (1973) ch 8).

BORMANN, E G *Theory and research in the communicative arts* (NY, Holt Rinehart & Winston, 1965).

BOULDING, K E *The image* (Ann Arbor, University of Michigan Press, 1956).

BOULDING, K E 'General systems theory: the skeleton of science' *Management science* 2 1956. 197-208; and *General systems* 1 1956. 11-17 (also in Buckley (1973) p 3-10).

BOULDING, K E 'The end is in sight for galloping science' *Washington post* September 6 1970 p B1 and B4.

BOURNE, L E *et al* *The psychology of thinking* (Englewood Cliffs, NJ, Prentice-Hall, 1970).

BRADBURY, F R, editor *Words and numbers: a student's guide to intellectual methods* (Edinburgh University Press, 1969).

BRAMLEY, G *A history of library education* (Bingley, 1969).

BRINTON, C *Ideas and men* (NY, Prentice-Hall, 1950).

BRONOWSKI, J *The ascent of man* (BBC, 1974).

BROOKES, B C 'R A F [airthorne] and the scope of information science' *Journal of documentation* 30 (2) June 1974. 139-152.

BROOME, A [*ie* M B LINE] 'The search for the ideal' *BLL Review* 2 (1) January 1974. 15-18.

BROWN, S C, editor *Physics 50 years later: as presented to the XIV General Assembly of the International Union of Pure and Applied Physics, 1972* (Washington, National Academy of Sciences, 1973).

BRUNER, J S *et al* *A study of thinking* (Wiley, 1956).

BRUNER, J S *The process of education* (NY, Vintage, 1960).

BRUNER, J S *On knowing: essays for the left hand* (Oxford University Press, 1962; Cambridge, Mass, Harvard University Press).

BRUNER, J S *Beyond the information given* (Allen & Unwin, 1974).

BRUNO, F J *The story of psychology* (NY, Holt Rinehart & Winston, 1972).

BRYAN, H 'The explosion in published information: myth or reality? *Australian library journal* 17 (1) December 1968. 389-401.

BUCKLEY, W *Modern systems research for the behavioral scientist: a sourcebook* (Chicago, Aldine, 1968).

BUCKLEY, W 'The systems approach to epistemology' in Klir (1972) p 188-202.

CALDWELL, W 'Libraries and information science' *Library association record* 72 (4) April 1970. 137-141.

CARNEY, T F *Content analysis: a technique for systematic evaluation from communications* (Batsford, 1972).

CARPENTER, E and McLUHAN, M, editors *Explorations in communication: an anthology* (Cape, 1970; first published 1960).

CARROLL, J B *Language and thought* (Prentice-Hall, 1964).

CASSIRER, E *The problem of knowledge* (New Haven, Yale University Press, 1950).

CAULFIELD, H J and LU, Sun *The applications of holography* (Wiley, 1970).

CAWKELL, A E 'Connections between engineering and science' *IEEE transactions on professional communication* PC-18 (2) June 1975. 71-73.

CHERNYI, A I, editor *Problems of information science* (Moscow, All-Union Institute for Scientific and Technical Information [VINITI], 1972) (FID 478).

CHERRY, H C *On human communication: a review, a survey and a criticism* 2nd edition (MIT Press, 1966).

CHISHOLM, R M *Theory of knowledge* (Prentice-Hall, 1966).

CHOMSKY, N *Chomsky: selected readings*, edited by J P B Allen and P van Buren (Oxford University Press, 1971).

CHURCHMAN, C West *The systems approach* (NY, Dell, 1968).

CIGÁNIK, M 'General system model of complex information' in Mikhailov (1969) vol 1, p 284-299.

CLAPP, V W *The future of the research library* (Urbana, University of Illinois Press, 1964).

CLARK, C *Population growth and land use* (Macmillan, 1967).

CLEVERDON, C 'Evaluation tests of information retrieval systems' [review] *Journal of documentation* 26 (1) March 1970. 55-67.

COLLIER, R J *et al Optical holography* (Academic Press, 1971).

COOKE, A *America* (BBC, 1974).

COX, P R *Demography* 4th edition (Cambridge University Press, 1970).

DANCE, F E X 'The concept of communication' *Journal of communication* 20, June 1970. 201-210.

DARLINGTON, C D *The evolution of man and society* (Allen & Unwin, 1969).

DEBONS, A *Information science: search for identity* (Dekker, 1974).

DEEVEY, E S 'The human population' *Scientific American* 203 (3) September 1960. 195-204.

DEREGOWSKI, J B 'Pictorial perception and culture' *Scientific American* 227 (5) November 1972. 82-8.

DRUCKER, P *The age of discontinuity* (Heinemann, 1969).

EASTLICK, J T, editor *The changing environment of libraries: papers delivered at the 1970-1971 Colloquium Series, Graduate School of Librarianship, University of Denver* (Chicago, ALA, 1971).

ECCLES, J 'The synapse' *Scientific American* 212 (1) January 1965. 56-66.

ELLIOT, C K *A guide to the documentation of psychology* (Bingley, 1971).

EMERY, F E *Systems thinking: selected readings* (Penguin, 1969).

ESCARPIT, R *Sociology of literature*, translated by Ernest Pick. 2nd edition (Frank Cass, 1971).

ESTES, W K *Learning and mental development* (Academic Press, 1970).

ETZIONI, A and ETZIONI, E *Social change: sources, patterns and consequences* (Basic, 1964).

EVANS, C R and ROBERTSON, A D J, editors *Brain physiology and psychology* (Butterworths, 1966).

178

FARRADANE, J [Book review] *Library Association record* 74 (1) January 1972. 19.

FISHMAN, M 'The transformational model of language and information retrieval' *Drexel library quarterly* 8 (2) April 1972. 193-200.

FOSHAY, A 'Education and the nature of a discipline' in WAETJEN, W B ed. *New dimensions of learning* (Washington, Association for Supervision and Curriculum Development, 1962).

FOSKETT, D J 'The intellectual and social challenge of the library service' *Library Association record* 70 (12) December 1968. 305-309.

FOSKETT, D J 'Informatics' *Journal of documentation* 26 (4) December 1970. 340-369.

FOSKETT, D J 'Information and general system theory' *Journal of librarianship* 4 (1) July 1972. 205-209.

FOSKETT, D J 'Some sociological aspects of formal systems for the communication of information' in Chernyi (1972).

FOSKETT, D J 'User psychology' in Lubbock (1972) p 385-396.

FOSKETT, D J 'Information science as an emergent discipline: educational implications' *Journal of librarianship* 5 (3) July 1973. 161-174.

FOSKETT, D J 'Information and general system theory' *Journal of librarianship* 6 (2) April 1974. 126-130.

FUGMANN, R 'Theoretical foundations of the IDC system: six postulates for information retrieval' *Aslib proceedings* 24 (2) February 1972. 123-138.

GARVEY, W D and GRIFFITH, B C 'Scientific communication as a social system' *Science* 157 (3797) September 1 1967. 1011-1016.

GARVEY, W D *et al* 'Communication in the physical and social sciences' *Science* 170 (3693) December 11 1970. 1166-1173.

GARVEY, W D *et al* 'The dynamic scientific information user' *Information storage and retrieval* 10 (3/4) March-April 1974. 115-131.

GAZZANIGA, M S 'The split brain in man' *Scientific American* 217 (2) August 1967. 24-9 (also in Held (1972) ch 4, and in Ornstein (1973) ch 7).

GAZZANIGA, M S *Fundamentals of psychology: an introduction* (Academic Press, 1973).

GERBNER, G 'Communication and social environment' *Scientific American* 227 (3) September 1972. 153-160.

GEYMONAT, G *Galileo Galilei* (McGraw-Hill, 1965).

GORN, S 'The computer and information sciences and the community of disciplines' *Behavioral science* 12 (6) November 1967. 433-452.

GOTTSCHALK, C M and DESMOND, W F 'Worldwide census of scientific and technical serials' *American documentation* 14 (3) July 1963. 188-194.

GRAY, J and PERRY, B *Scientific information* (Oxford University Press, 1975).

GREEN, J C 'The information explosion: real or imaginary?' *Science* 144 (3619) May 8 1964. 647-8.

GREENE, J *Psycholinguistics: Chomsky and psychology* (Penguin Education, 1972).

GREGORY, R L *The intelligent eye* (Weidenfeld and Nicholson, 1970).

GREGORY, R L *Concepts and mechanisms of perception* (Duckworth, 1974).

GRUSKY, O and MILLER, G A, editors *The sociology of organizations: basic studies* (Collier-Macmillan, 1970).

GUILFORD, J P *Intelligence, creativity and their educational implications* (San Diego, California, Knapp, 1968).

GURVITCH, C *Social frameworks of knowledge* (Blackwell, 1971).

HAGSTROM, W H *The scientific community* (NY, Basic, 1965).

HALL, E T *Silent language* (NY, Doubleday, 1959).

HANDLIN, O 'Science and technology in popular culture' *Daedalus* 94 (1) Winter, 1965. 156-170.

HANSON, C W *Introduction to science-information work* (Aslib, 1971).

HARMON, G *Human memory and knowledge* (Greenwood, 1973) (Contributions in librarianship and information science, 6).

HARRÉ, R *The principles of scientific thinking* (Macmillan, 1970).

HASLERUD, G M *Transfer, memory and creativity* (Minneapolis, University of Minnesota Press, 1972).

HAYAKAWA, S *Language in thought and action* 2nd edition (Allen & Unwin, 1965).

HAYES, R M 'Information science in librarianship' *Libri* 19 (3) 1969. 216-236 and *IFLA communications* 1969, no 1, 216-236.

HAYS, S 'New possibilities for American history' in Lipset (1968) p 181-227.

HEBB, D O *Textbook of psychology* 3rd edition (Saunders, 1972).

HELD, R and RICHARDS, W, editors *Perception: mechanisms and models* (Reading, Mass, Freeman, 1972) (*Scientific American* reprints).

HEMPEL, C G *Philosophy of natural science* (Prentice-Hall, 1966).

HESSE, M *The structure of scientific inference* (Macmillan, 1973).

HETHERINGTON, N S 'Adriaan van Maanen and internal motions in spiral nebulae: a historical review' *Quarterly journal of the Royal Astronomical Society* 13 (1) March 1972. 25-39.

HILGARD, E R *et al Introduction to psychology* 5th edition (NY, Harcourt Brace Jovanovich, 1971) (Open University set book), (6th edition, 1975).

HIMSWORTH, H *The development and organization of scientific knowledge* (Heinemann, 1970).

HINTIKKA, J and SUPPES, P, editors *Information and inference* (Dordrecht, Reidel, 1970) (Synthese Library).

HIRST, P H *Knowledge and the curriculum: a collection of philosophical papers* (Routledge & Kegan Paul, 1974).

HOFFMAN, R *Languages, minds and knowledge* (Allen & Unwin, 1970).

HOIJER, H, editor *Language in culture: conference on the interrelations of language and other aspects of culture* (Chicago, University of Chicago Press, 1954).

HOLTON, G 'Scientific research and scholarship: notes towards the design of proper scales' *Daedalus* 94 (2) Spring 1962. 362-399.

HUTCHINS, W J Languages of indexing and classification: a linguistic study of structures and functions (Stevenage, Peregrinus, 1975).

HUXLEY, J *Heredity east and west: Lysenko and world science* (NY, Schuman, 1949; reprinted Kraus, 1969).

INFORMATICS I: Proceedings of a conference held by the Aslib Coordinate Indexing Group, 1973 (Aslib, 1974).

INNIS, H A *The bias of communication* (Toronto, University of Toronto Press, 1964).

JEVONS, F R *Science observed: science as a social and intellectual activity* (Allen & Unwin, 1973).

JOHNSON, C and BRIGGS, E 'Holography as applied to information storage and retrieval systems' *ASIS journal* 22 (3) May-June 1971. 187-192.

JOHNSON-LAIRD, P N *et al* 'Memory for words' *Nature* 251 (5477) October 25 1974. 704-5.

JONES, C *et al* 'The characteristics of the literature used by historians' *Journal of librarianship* 4 (3) July 1972. 137-156.

JONES, K P 'The environment of classification, part II: how we classify' *ASIS journal* 25 (1) January-February 1974. 44-51.

JONES, K Sparck and KAY, M *Linguistics and information science* (Academic Press, 1973).

JORDAN, D S *The stability of truth* (NY, Holt, 1911).

KATZ, D and KAHN, R L *The social psychology of organizations* (Wiley, 1966).

KELLEY, H J 'Entropy of knowledge' *Philosophy of science* 36 (2) June 1969. 178-196.

KEMP, D A 'Relevance, pertinence and information system development' *Information storage and retrieval* 10 (1) 1974. 37-47.

KENDLER, H H 'The concept of a concept' in Melton (1964) p 211-236.

KENNEDY, A and WILKES, A, editors *Studies in long-term memory*
(Wiley, 1975).

KIMBER, R T *Automation in libraries* 2nd edition (Pergamon, 1974).

KING, D W and BRYANT, E C *The evaluation of information services
and products* (Washington, Information Resources Press, 1971).

KISSEL, G and WERSIG, G 'The overall framework of information
science research' *IATUL proceedings* 6 (2) May 1972. 54-6.

KLAUSMEIER, H J and HARRIS, C W, editors *Analyses of concept
learning* (Academic Press, 1966).

KLIR, G J, editor *Trends in general system theory* (NY, Wiley-
Interscience, 1972).

KOCHEN, M, editor *The growth of knowledge* (Wiley, 1967).

KOCHEN, M 'Stability in the growth of knowledge' *American
documentation* 20 (3) July 1969. 186-197.

KOCHEN, M *Integrative mechanisms in literature growth* (Greenwood,
1973) (Contributions in librarianship and information science, 5).

KOCK, V E *Lasers and holography: an introduction to coherent optics*
(Heinemann, 1972).

KOESTLER, A *Act of creation* (NY, Macmillan, 1966).

KORNER, S *Fundamental questions of philosophy: one philosopher's
answers* (Penguin, 1973).

KUHN, T S *The structure of scientific revolutions* 2nd edition (University
of Chicago Press, 1970).

LAKATOS, I and MUSGRAVE, A, editors *Criticism and the growth of
knowledge* (Cambridge University Press, 1970).

LAKOFF, S A, editor *Knowledge and power* (NY, Free Press, 1966).

LANDHEER, B *Social functions of libraries* (NY, Scarecrow, 1957).

LANGRIDGE, D *The universe of knowledge* (College Park, University
of Maryland, School of Library and Information Sciences, 1969)
(Student contribution series, 2).

LANGRIDGE, D *Approach to classification* (Bingley, 1973).

LARSEN, P S *A bibliography of PRECIS* (Aalborg, Royal School of
Librarianship, 1976).

LASZLO, E *Introduction to systems philosophy* (NY, Gordon &
Breach, 1972).

LEE, D 'Codifications of reality: lineal and non-lineal' *Psychosomatic
medicine* 12 (2) 1950. 89-97 (also in Carpenter (1970) p 136-154
and in Ornstein (1973) p 128-142).

LEE, D S 'Scientific method as a stage process' *Dialectica 22* (1) 1968. 328-44.

LESK, M E and SALTON, G 'Relevance assessments and retrieval system evaluations' *Information storage and retrieval* 4 (4) December 1968. 343-359.

LICKLIDER, J C R 'A crux in scientific and technical communication' *American psychologist* 21 (11) November 1966. 1044-1055.

LINDESMITH, A R and STRAUSS, A L *Social psychology* 3rd edition (Holt, Rinehart & Winston, 1968).

LINDGREN, H C and BYRNE, D *Psychology: an introduction to a behavioral science* 3rd edition (Wiley, 1971)

LINDGREN, H C *Introduction to social psychology* 2nd edition (Wiley, 1973).

LINDSAY, P H and NORMAN, D A *Human information processing: an introduction to psychology* (Academic Press, 1972).

LINE, M B 'On the design of information systems for human beings' *Aslib proceedings* 22 (7) July 1970. 320-335.

LIPSET, S M and HOFSTADTER, R *Sociology and history: methods* (Basic, 1968).

LISTON, D M and SCHOENE, M L 'A systems approach to the design of information systems' *ASIS journal* 22 (2) March-April 1971. 115-122.

LOOSJES, Th P *On documentation of scientific literature* (Butterworths, 1967).

LOSEE, J *A historical introduction to the philosophy of science* (Oxford University Press, 1972).

LOTKA, A J *Elements of physical biology* (Williams & Wilkins, 1925; reissued NY, Dover, 1956, with title *Elements of mathematical biology*).

LUBBOCK, G, editor *International conference on training for information work, Rome, 1971 Proceedings* (Rome, Italian National Information Institute, 1972; The Hague, International Federation for Documentation).

LYONS, J *Chomsky* (Fontana/Collins, 1970).

McGARRY, K J *Communications* (Bingley, 1975).

MACHLUP, F *Production and distribution of knowledge in the United States* (Princeton, Princeton University Press, 1962).

MACK, R W and PEASE, J *Sociology and social life* 5th edition (Van Nostrand, 1973).

MACKAY, D M *Information, mechanism and meaning* (MIT Press, 1969).

183

MADDOX, B *Beyond Babel: new directions in communications* (Deutsch, 1972).

MAGEE, B *Modern British philosophy* (Secker, 1971).

MAGEE, B *Popper* (Collins/Fontana, 1973) (see also *Sunday times* (magazine) May 27 1973. 33-43).

MALTBY, A *Sayers' manual of classification for librarians* 5th edition (Deutsch, 1975).

MANDLER, G 'Organization and memory' in Spence (1967) p 327-371.

MANIS, M *Cognitive processes* (Belmont, California, Brookes/Cole, 1966).

MASON, S F *Main currents of scientific thought: a history of the sciences* (Routledge & Kegan Paul, 1956; NY, Abelard-Schuman).

MEADOWS, A J *Communications in science* (Butterworths, 1974).

MEDAWAR, P B *The art of the soluble* (Penguin, 1969).

MEDVEDEV, Z A *The rise and fall of T D Lysenko* (Columbia University Press, 1969).

MEIER, R 'Information input overload: features of growth in communications oriented institutions' *Libri* 13 (1) 1961. 1-44.

MELTON, A W, editor *Categories of human learning* (Academic Press, 1964).

MENARD, H W *Science: growth and change* (Cambridge, Mass, Harvard University Press, 1971).

MEREDITH, G P 'Thoughts on communication' *Journal of documentation* 12 (3) September 1956. 171-182.

MEREDITH, P *Instruments of communication: an essay on scientific writing* (Pergamon, 1966).

MERTA, A 'Informal communication in science' in Chernyi (1972) p 34-52.

MERTON, R K *The sociology of science: theoretical and empirical investigations* (University of Chicago Press, 1973).

METZ, W D [Report of address by A Sandage] *Science* 178 (4061) November 10 1972. 601.

MEZRICH, R 'A medium for the message' *Industrial research* 11 (11) 1969. 58-60.

MIKHAILOV, A and GILYAREVSKII, R S *Introductory course on information/documentation* (Paris, UNESCO, 1970) (COM/WS/147).

MIKHAILOV, A I *et al*, editors *International forum on informatics (1968?)* (Moscow, VINITI, 1969). 2 vols.

MILLER, G A 'The magic number seven, plus or minus two: or, some limits on our capacity for processing information' *Psychological review* 63 (2) March 1956. 81-97 (see also Evans (1966) p 174-200; Miller (1968) p 14-44; and elsewhere).

MILLER, G A *Psychology: the science of mental life* (Hutchinson, 1966).

MILLER, G A *The psychology of communication: seven essays* (Allen Lane/Penguin, 1968).

MILLER, P R *Sense and symbol* (Staples Press, 1969).

MILSUM, J H *Positive feedback: a general systems approach to positive/ negative feedback and mutual causality* (Pergamon, 1968).

MINTER, R L 'A denotative and connotative study in communication' *Journal of communication* 18 (1) March 1968. 26-36.

MITROFF, I I *The subjective side of science: a philosophical enquiry into the psychology of the Apollo Moon scientists* (Amsterdam, Elsevier, 1974).

MONTGOMERY, C A 'Linguistics and information science' *ASIS journal* 23 (3) May-June 1972. 195-219.

MONTGOMERY, E B, editor *Foundations of access to knowledge: a symposium* (Syracuse, NY, Syracuse University, 1968).

MORRIS, C *Signs, language and behavior* (NY, Prentice-Hall, 1946).

MORTENSEN, C D *Communication: the study of human interaction* (McGraw-Hill, 1972) (also *Study guide*. McGraw-Hill, 1972).

MUNN, N L *Introduction to psychology* (Harrap, 1962).

MUNN, N L *Psychology: fundamentals of human adjustment* (Harrap, 1966).

MURPHY, G and KOVACH, J K *Historical introduction to modern psychology* 6th edition (Routledge & Kegan Paul, 1972).

NELSON, C E and POLLOCK, D K, editors *Communication among scientists and engineers* (Lexington, Heath, 1970).

NORMAN, D A *Memory and attention* (Wiley, 1969).

OLBY, R *The path to the double helix* (Macmillan, 1974).

ORNSTEIN, R E *The psychology of consciousness* (NY, Viking, 1972).

ORNSTEIN, R E *The nature of human consciousness: a book of readings* (San Francisco, Freeman; NY, Viking, 1973).

OTTEN, K and DEBONS, A 'Towards a metascience of information: informatology' *ASIS journal* 21 (1) January-February 1970. 89-94.

PANTIN, C F A *The relations between the sciences* (Cambridge University Press, 1968) (Tarner Lectures, 1959).

PARRY, J *Psychology of human communication* (University of London Press, 1967).

PASSMAN, S *Scientific and technological communication* (Pergamon, 1969).

PENLAND, P R *Communication for librarians* (University of Pittsburgh, 1971).

PETYT, K M 'Some recent approaches to the study of meaning' *Aslib proceedings* 24 (7) July 1972. 412-418.

PIAGET, J *Logic and psychology* (NY, Basic, 1957).

PIAGET, J *Psychology and epistemology: towards a theory of knowledge* (Allen Lane/Penguin, 1972).

PLATT, J R 'The fifth need of man' *Horizon* 1 July 1959. 106.

POHL, H 'Information science—fiction or fact?' *American documentation* 16 (2) April 1965. 69-72.

POLANYI, M *Personal knowledge* (University of Chicago Press, 1958).

POOL, I de Sola *et al*, editors. *Handbook of communication* (Chicago, Rand McNally, 1973).

POPPER, K R *Conjectures and refutations: the growth of scientific knowledge* 2nd edition revised. (Routledge & Kegan Paul, 1965).

POPPER, K R *The logic of scientific discovery* 3rd revised edition (Hutchinson, 1968).

POPPER, K R *Objective knowledge: an evolutionary approach* (Clarendon Press, 1972).

POTTER, S *Language in the modern world* (Penguin, 1960).

PREMACK, A J and PREMACK, D 'Teaching language to an ape' *Scientific American* 227 (4) October 1972. 92-99, 128.

PRIBRAM, K H *On the biology of learning* (NY, Harcourt, Brace & World, 1969).

PRIBRAM, K H *Languages and physiology: experimental paradoxes and principles in neuropsychology* (Prentice-Hall, 1971).

PRICE, D J de Solla *Little science, big science* (NY, Columbia University Press, 1963).

PRICE, D J de Solla *Science since Babylon* enlarged edition (Yale University Press, 1975).

RANGANATHAN, S R *Prolegomena to library classification* 3rd edition (Asia Publishing House, 1967).

RAPAPORT, D *Organization and pathology of thought* (NY, Columbia University Press, 1951).

RESTLE, F *Animal behavior and human cognition* (McGraw-Hill, 1975).

REUCK, A de, and KNIGHT, J, editors *Communication in science* (Churchill, 1967).

REYWARD, W B 'Libraries as organizations' *College and research libraries* 30 (4) July 1969. 312-326.

RICHARDSON, E C *Classification, theoretical and practical* 3rd edition (Hamden, Connecticut, Shoestring Press, 1964 ; facsimile reprint, first published 1930).

RICHMAN, F *et al. Mathematics for the liberal arts student* 2nd edition (Monterrey, California, Brookes/Cole, 1973).

RIDER, F *The scholar and the future of the research library* (NY, Hadham Press, 1944).

RIESMAN, D 'The oral and written traditions' in Carpenter (1970) p 109-116.

ROBINSON, F *et al Systems analysis in libraries* (Oriel Press, 1969) (Symplegades, no 2).

ROBINSON, J O *The psychology of visual illusion* (Hutchinson, 1972).

ROMMETWEIT, R *Words, meanings and messages: theory and experiments in psycholinguistics* (Academic Press, 1968).

ROSENBLITH, W A 'The brain' *International science and technology* September, 1967. 34-46, 100.

ROWAN, J *The science of you* (Davis-Poynter, 1973) (Psychological aspects of society, Book 1).

RUBINSTEIN, H *Some problems of meaning in natural language* (in Pool (1973) p. 27-45).

RUSSELL, B *Human knowledge: its scope and limits* (Allen & Unwin, 1948).

SAMPSON, E E *Social psychology and contemporary society* (Wiley, 1971).

SARACEVIC, T *Introduction to information science* (NY, Bowker, 1970).

SAUNDERS, W L 'The development of libraries as a key factor in communication' in *Proceedings of the Public Libraries Conference, Blackpool, 1971* (Library Association, 1972) p 17-23.

SCIENTIFIC AMERICAN 227 (3) September 1972 'Communication' (issue devoted entirely to this subject; 11 papers).

SHELDON, E B *Indicators of social change: concepts and measurements* (NY, Russell Sage Foundation, 1968).

SHERA, J H *Documentation and the organization of knowledge* (Crosby Lockwood, 1966).

SHERA, J H *Sociological foundations of librarianship* (Asia Publishing House, 1970) (Sarada Ranganathan Lectures, vol 3, 1967).

SHERA, J H *The foundations of education for librarianship* (Wiley, 1972).

SHERA, J H 'Mechanization, librarianship and the bibliographic enterprise' *Journal of documentation* 30 (2) June 1974. 153-169.

SILVERMAN, D *The theory of organisations: a sociological framework* (Heinemann, 1974).

SINGER, C J *A short history of scientific ideas to 1900* (Oxford University Press, 1959).

SKELTON, B 'Scientists and social scientists as information users: a comparison of the results of science user studies with the investigation into information requirements of the social sciences' *Journal of librarianship* 5 (2) April 1973. 138-156.

SMITH, A G, editor *Communications and culture: readings on the codes of human interaction* (NY, Holt, Rinehart & Winston, 1966).

SNOW, C P *The two cultures; and, A second look* (Cambridge University Press, 1964).

SPENCE, K W and SPENCE, J T, editors *The psychology of learning and motivation: advances in theory and research* (Academic Press, 1967).

SPITZ, H H 'The role of input organization in the learning and memory of mental retardates' *International review of research on mental retardation* (N R Ellis, editor) 2 1966. 29-56.

STAMPER, R *Information in business and administrative systems* (Batsford, 1973).

STEBBING, L S *A modern elementary logic* 5th edition revised (Methuen, 1952).

STENT, G S 'Prematurity and uniqueness in scientific discovery' *Scientific American* 227 (6) December 1972. 84-93, 128.

SWANSON, D R *The intellectual foundations of library education* (Chicago, University of Chicago Press, 1965).

SWANSON, R W 'The information business is a people business' *Information storage and retrieval* 6 (4) October 1970. 351-361.

SWEENEY, F, editor *The knowledge explosion: liberation and limitation* (NY, Farrar, Strauss & Giroux, 1966).

TAYLOR, R S 'A structure for change in education and research in the information/communication field' *Proceedings of the American Society for Information Science* 2 1973. 147-153.

THAYER, L 'On theory building in communication: some conceptual issues' *Journal of communication* 13 (4) 1963. 217-235.

THOMAS, P A *Task analysis of library operations* (Aslib, 1971). (Aslib Occasional Publications, no 8).

THOMPSON, R F *Physiological psychology* (Reading, Mass, Freeman, 1972).

THOMSON, R *The psychology of thinking* (Penguin, 1959).

THOMSON, R *The Pelican history of psychology* (Penguin, 1968).

THORPE, W H *Animal nature and human nature* (Methuen, 1975).

TOFFLER, A *Future shock* (Bodley Head, 1970; NY, Bantam).

VICKERY, B C *Faceted classification: a guide to construction and use of special schemes* (Aslib, 1960).

VICKERY, B C 'Statistics of scientific and technical articles' *Journal of documentation* 24 (3) September 1968. 192-194.

VICKERY, B C *Information systems* (Butterworths, 1973).

VINACKE, W E *Psychology of thinking* (McGraw-Hill, 1952).

VOOS, H 'The information explosion: or, redundancy reduces the charge' *College and research libraries* 32 (1) January 1971. 7-14.

VYGOTSKY, L S *Thought and language* (Wiley, 1962).

WATANABE, S *Knowing and guessing* (Wiley, 1969).

WATSON, J D *The double helix* (Weidenfeld and Nicholson, 1968).

WATSON, L E *et al* 'Sociology and information science' *Journal of librarianship* 5 (4) October 1973. 270-283.

WATT, I *The rise of the novel: Studies in Defoe, Richardson and Fielding* (Chatto & Windus, 1957; reprinted Pelican, 1976).

WEATHERALL, M *Scientific method* (English Universities Press, 1968).

WEISS, P 'Knowledge: a growth process' *Science* 131 (3415) June 10 1960. 1716-1719, and *Proceedings of the American Philosophical Society* 104 (2) April 1960. 242-247 (also in Kochen (1967) p 209-215).

WELLISCH, H 'From information science to informatics: a terminological investigation'. *Journal of librarianship* 4 (3) July 1972. 157-187.

WERNER, H and KAPLAN, B *Symbol formation* (Wiley, 1963).

WESSON, P 'The position against continental drift' *Quarterly journal of the Royal Astronomical Society* 11 (4) December 1970. 312-340.

WHITE, L A *The evolution of culture: the development of civilization to the fall of Rome* (McGraw-Hill, 1959).

WHORF, B L *Language, thought and reality* (Wiley, 1956).

WILSON, J Tuzo 'The physical study of the Earth and the scientific revolution it has caused' in Brown (1973) p 37-61.

WORTMANN, P M and GREENBERG, L D 'Coding, recording and decoding of hierarchical information in long-term memory' *Journal of verbal learning and verbal behaviour* 10 (3) 1971. 234-243.

WYATT, H V 'How history has blended' *Nature* 249 (5460) June 28 1974. 803-805.

ZIMAN, J M *Public Knowledge: an essay concerning the social dimensions of science* (Cambridge University Press, 1968).

ZIMAN, J M 'The light of knowledge: new lamps for old' *Aslib proceedings* 22 (5) May 1970. 186-200.

INDEX

The facilities of a computer were used to enable the author to compile the index. The resultant print-out is reproduced here in its original form.